SUGARCRAFT
FLOWER ARRANGING

ALAN DUNN'S
SUGARCRAFT
FLOWER ARRANGING

NEW
HOLLAND

First published in 2009 by New Holland Publishers (UK) Ltd
London • Cape Town • Sydney • Auckland

Garfield House
86–88 Edgware Road
London W2 2EA
United Kingdom

80 McKenzie Street
Cape Town 8001
South Africa

Unit 1
66 Gibbes Street
Chatswood
NSW 2067
Australia

218 Lake Road
Northcote
Auckland
New Zealand

ISBN   978 1 84773 441·9

Senior Editor Corinne Masciocchi
Designer Isobel Gillan
Photographer Sue Atkinson
Production Laurence Poos
Editorial Direction Rosemary Wilkinson

2 4 6 8 10 9 7 5 3 1

Reproduction by PDQ Digital Media Solutions Ltd., UK.
Printed and bound by Craft Print International, Singapore

CONTENTS

Introduction

For me, floral arrangements and sprays are an essential part of designing and decorating a celebration or wedding cake. I find that many of the people I teach are happy to make sugar flowers but find choosing what flowers and foliage to use and figuring out colour combinations difficult, and the art of flower arranging a challenge. I actually enjoy the process of colouring and arranging more than making the sugar flowers - it is the process that drives my passion for creating floral displays for cakes, exhibitions as well as my books too.

When I first started cake decorating and making sugar flowers - more than 20 odd years ago now - I was taught by Margaret Morland and Tombi Peck not only how to make sugar flowers but to assemble them into sprays too. The crescent-shaped spray and posy that they taught me have been invaluable - they have been the basis of many of the sprays I have used on cakes over the years. After my initial introduction to wiring sprays of sugar flowers, I then went on to buy as many floristry and flower-arranging books as I could. Following many of the guidelines in these books, which were often aimed at commercial florists, I have been able to gradually create a style of my own. I have gone through many trends and phases over the years, often using masses and masses of flowers and foliage to create large displays. I now prefer to use fewer elements in my designs as the process of creating elaborate designs can prove to be too time-consuming to reproduce regularly and the finished result is often way out of the price range of a paying customer.

I am still very inspired by the work of florists and flower arrangers and still get great pleasure from buying floristry books, visiting florists and seeing the odd fresh flower demonstration, not to mention buying fresh flowers to replicate in both sugar and cold porcelain. However, it is important to remember that sugar and cold porcelain flowers have their own appeal and that they have to work well as part of a cake design.

In this book I have presented a variety of designs to guide both the novice and the more experienced flower maker to create interesting sprays, bouquets and arrangements. I hope that my work will inspire everyone to create and develop a unique and individual style. Many of the floristry guidelines that I have picked up along the way are used in these designs but remember they are only guidelines! Essentially you are just trying to create a balanced design that pleases the eye and you must remember that often sugar flowers will just not bend and fit into many of the more regimental fresh floral designs. So, it is best to allow your creative juices to flow and react to your gut instinct when creating floral designs for cakes.

Equipment

There is a huge array of equipment available, but you actually just need a few basic pieces. I have also added some information here on ribbons, wires, beads etc.

Non-stick board and rolling pin

These are essential pieces of equipment. Avoid white boards as they strain the eyes too much. Some boards can be very shiny, making it difficult to frill petals against them. If this is the case simply roughen up the surface using some fine glass paper prior to use or alternatively turn the board over and use the back which is often less shiny. I always use a thin layer of white vegetable fat rubbed into the surface, removing most of the excess with dry kitchen paper – this stops the paste sticking to the board and also makes you check each time to see if it is clean from food colour.

Scissors, pliers and wire cutters

Fine embroidery and curved scissors are very useful for cutting fine petals, thread and ribbons. Larger florists' scissors are handy for cutting wires. Small, fine-nose pliers are essential. Good quality pliers from electrical supply shops are best – they are expensive but worth the investment. Electrical wire cutters are useful for cutting heavier wires.

Tweezers

It is important to use fine-angle tweezers without ridges (or teeth). They are useful for pinching ridges on petals and holding very fine petals and stamens. You will also find them helpful when arranging flowers to push smaller items into difficult, tight areas of an arrangement or spray.

Foam pads

These are great to place petals and leaves on while you soften the edges – especially if you have hot hands that tend to dissolve the petals as you are working them. Prior to buying this product check that it has a good surface, as some have rough, open-textured surfaces that will both tear the edges of your petals or leave marks on them. I like either the large, blue pad called a Billy's Block or the yellow Celpad.

Wires and floristry tape

Wires are available in many colours – I buy mostly white paper-covered wires, preferring to colour or tape over as I work. The quality varies between brands. The most consistent in quality are the Japanese Sunrise

Wires. These are available from 35-gauge (very fine but rare) to 24-gauge (thicker). Floristry tape is used in the construction of stems and bouquets. They contain a glue that is released when the tape is stretched. I am quite fussy about which tape I buy. I use mainly nile green tape from the Lion Brand tape company. White, beige, brown, twig, yellow, pink and dark red can also be useful. Some of the brands of tape are very harsh to work with – they have a strong, crayon-type smell to them and should be avoided at all costs as they will hurt your fingers as you work with them.

Tape shredder

Some cake decorators hate this gadget. I find that if it is used properly it saves a lot of time and energy. The tool contains three razor blades to cut floristry tape into quarter widths. I have a couple of tape shredders and have removed two blades from one of them so that it cuts the tape into half widths. It is often best to use a tiny amount of cold cream rubbed onto the blades with a cotton bud and also a little onto the lid that presses against the blades – this will help the

tape run smoothly against the blades as it can often stick due to an excess of glue left behind from the tape. It is also wise to remove any excess build-up of glue from the blades using fine-nose pliers, and also to replace the blades regularly. Handle with care at all times.

Paintbrushes

Good quality, synthetic brushes or synthetic-blend brushes from art shops are best. I use mainly short, flat, not too soft bristle brushes for applying layers of food colour dusts to flowers and leaves. It is best to keep brushes for certain colours so you don't have to wash them after each use. I use finer sable or synthetic-blend brushes for painting fine lines or detail spots onto petals.

Flower cutters

Flowers may be made using templates or freestyle techniques, however, the use of plastic and metal cutters creates speed and consistent accuracy of shape. I use mostly metal cutters as I can alter the shape of these if required to suit flowers other than the one it was intended to make. Many of the more interesting leaf shapes with serrated edges and intricate designs are available in plastic.

Leaf and petal veiners

These are made from food-grade silicone rubber. They are very useful for creating natural petal and leaf texturing to sugarwork. The moulds are made using mostly real plant material to give the finished sugar flower a realistic finish. As with the flower cutters, there is a huge selection of commercial veiners to choose from.

Stamens

There is a vast selection of commercial stamens available from cake decorating shops. I use mainly fine white and seed-head stamens, which I then colour using powder colours.

Posy picks

These are made from food-grade plastic and are available in various sizes. They are used to hold the handle of a spray or bouquet of flowers into the cake. The food-grade plastic protects the cake from contamination from the wires and floristry tape used in the construction of the floral spray. Never push wires directly into a cake.

Modelling tools

Metal ball tools (Cc) (Celcakes)
These are available in plastic or metal. I find the latter more useful as the weight of the tool means that less effort is needed to soften/thin the

edges of the paste. Use the tool to rub or roll the edge of the paste, positioning it half on the petal/leaf edge and half on your hand or foam pad the petal is resting against. They can also be used to 'cup' or hollow out petals to form interesting shapes.

Plain-edge cutting wheel (PME) and sharp scalpel
This cutting wheel is rather like a double-sided small pizza wheel. It is great for cutting out quick petals and leaves and also for adding division lines to buds. A sharp scalpel is also essential for marking veins, adding texture, and cutting out petal shapes too.

Dresden/veining tool (J) (PME)
The fine end of this tool is great for adding central veins to petals or leaves, and the broader end can be used for working the edges of a leaf to give a serrated effect or a 'double frilled' effect on the edges of petals. Simply press the tool against the paste repeatedly to create a tight frilled effect or pull the tool against the paste on a non-stick board to create

EQUIPMENT

serrations. The fine end of the tool can also be used to cut into the edge of leaves and to cut and flick finer serrated-edge leaves. I use a black tool by Jem for finer, smaller leaves and flowers, and the larger yellow PME tool for larger flowers.

Ceramic Tools (HP – Holly Products)
I use a smooth ceramic tool for curling the edges of petals and hollowing out throats of small flowers as well as using it as a mini rolling pin. The silk veining tool is wonderful for creating delicate veins and frills to petal edges.

Celsticks (Cc – Celcakes)
There are four sizes of these small rolling pin-type tools. As well as being great for rolling out small petals and leaves to create thick ridges, the pointed end of the tool is great for opening up the centre of 'hat'-type flowers. The rounded end can be used in the same way as a ball tool to soften edges and hollow out petals.

Glue
Non-toxic glue sticks can be bought from stationery or art shops and are great for fixing ribbon to the board edge. Always make sure that the glue does not come into direct contact with the cake. I use a non-toxic hi-tack craft glue to attach stamens to the end of wires. I feel that no harm is being done sticking inedible items together with another inedible item. However, the glue should not come into direct contact with the sugar petals as it will dissolve them.

Florists' staysoft
This is basically the soft modelling material that I used to play with as a child. It can be bought in blocks of various colours from florists' suppliers, art shops and some cake decorating shops too. This medium should be placed into a vase or onto a thin board to protect the cake surface. As the name implies, the medium stays fairly firm but soft which is great for arranging sugar flowers into as the flowers can be removed and rearranged if needed.

Kitchen-paper ring formers
These basic formers are useful for drying petals that require a cupped shape. The open loops allow the flowerpaste to breathe so that it dries faster than if placed into a plastic or other type of former. To make, cut strips of kitchen paper and twist back onto themselves and then tie into a loop. Larger formers can be made by cutting the kitchen paper sheet in half diagonally and then twisting – these are useful for much larger petals that require support while drying.

Ribbons, braids and paper-covered wires
These are an essential part of cake decorating – they are used simply to decorate the base of a cake, to edge a cake board or wired into loops to add into floral displays. They provide the decorator with a very quick and effective addition to a cake design. The colour of most of these can be changed to match the colour of the

flowers you are using on the cake. Simply rub an anti-bacterial wipe into some petal dust and then run it quickly and firmly along the ribbon to change its colour. This can be very useful when working late at night when you can't run out to the shops to buy more ribbon. I keep a good supply of paler ribbons that can be altered easily. Double-coloured satin ribbon can also be very useful – it means you always have something that could be suitable for the design you are working on. You will find buying ribbons and trims quite addictive, but it does make life easier if you have a good variety of colours and textures to work with.

Other decorative items
These include beads, metallic wires in various strengths and colours, beaded wires, decorative florists' mesh and crimped reel wires. There are also things like coloured sisal fibre, which can be used to hide the mechanics of an arrangement or even rolled into balls or formed into heart shapes, etc. and tied with decorative metallic wires which can be added to your displays too. I enjoy adding these elements to my sprays and arrangements. They all catch the light well and add interest. However, care must be taken to use these items on pieces that will be removed from the cake prior to cutting. There has been a trend in recent years for pushing crystals and beads directly into the surface of an iced cake – while this can look pretty it is an extremely dangerous practice.

Techniques

These are some of the more important techniques that you'll use time and time again when making sugar flowers and cold porcelain flowers.

Wiring petals and leaves

1 Knead a piece of flowerpaste and form roughly into the shape of the petal or leaf you are making. Press it down against a non-stick board to flatten it slightly. Use a celstick or rolling pin to roll the paste, leaving a ridge for the wire. Try to create a tapered ridge, angling the pin slightly so that the ridge is thicker at the base of the petal or leaf. The thickness and length of the ridge will depend on the size of the petal/leaf you are making. There are also boards available commercially which have grooves in them that create a similar ridged effect when the paste is rolled over them.

2 Cut out the petal/leaf shape using scalpel or plain-edge cutting wheel, leaving the ridge to run down the centre. If you are using a cutter, lift up the shape and place it onto a light dusting of cornflour and then press firmly with the cutter. Scrub it against the paste and the board so that the shape remains slightly stuck in the cutter. This will enable you to rub the edge of the cutter to create a cleaner cut edge, removing any fuzzy bits!

3 Moisten the wire very slightly – too much moistness will result in the paper coming off the wire and also slow down the drying process. Hold the ridge firmly between your finger and thumb, and hold the wire in the other hand very close to the end of the wire that is being inserted into the shape. Push the wire in gradually so that it supports a third to half the length. Continue forming the shape following the instructions for each individual flower or leaf.

Working with flowerpaste

The paste should be well kneaded before you start to roll out or model it into a flower shape, otherwise it has a tendency to dry out and crack around the edges. This is an air-drying paste so when you are not using it make sure it is well wrapped in a plastic bag. If you have cut out lots of petals cover them over with a plastic bag.

Egg white

You will need fresh egg white to stick petals together and to alter the consistency of flowerpaste if it is too dry. There are commercially available edible glues which can be used instead but I find that these tend to dissolve the sugar slightly before allowing it to dry, resulting in weak petals.

White vegetable fat

I use this to grease the non-stick board and then wipe it off with dry kitchen paper. This not only conditions the board, but also removes excess food colour from the previous flower-making session. You can also add a tiny amount of white fat to the paste if it is very sticky – however, you must not add too much as it will make the paste short and slow down the drying process too much. Don't leave too much fat on the board as greasy patches will show up on the petals when you start to apply the dry dusting colours.

Cornflour bag

Cornflour is a life-saver when the flowerpaste is sticky. It is best to make a cornflour bag using disposable nappy liners! Fold a couple of layers of nappy liners together and add a good tablespoon of cornflour on top. Tie into a bag then use it to lightly dust the paste prior to rolling it out and also on petals and leaves before they are placed into a veiner.

Colouring

Listed below are the forms of colour available to the cake decorator. If you are attaching an edible decoration onto a cake, check that the colours are edible and not just non-toxic.

Paste food colours

I prefer to work with white or a very pale base colour and then create a stronger finished colour using powder food colours. I add paste colours into sugarpaste to cover the cakes, but even then I am not a huge fan of strongly coloured cake coverings. It is best to mix up a small amount of sugar- or flowerpaste with paste food colour, then add this smaller amount to a larger amount of paste – this prevents you adding too much colour to the entire amount of paste.

Petal dusts

These food colour dusts are wonderful for creating very soft and also very intense colouring to finished flowers. The dusts can be mixed together to form different colours or brushed on in layers, which creates more interest and depth to the finished flower or leaf. White petal dust can be added to soften the colours – some cake decorators add cornflour, however, this weakens the gum content of the dust, often causing a streaky effect to the petal. If you are trying to create strong, bold colours, dust the surface of the flowerpaste while it is still fairly pliable or at the leather-hard stage. A paint can also be made by adding clear alcohol (isopropyl) to the dust.

This is good for adding spots and finer details. You can also add these dusts to melted cocoa butter to make a paint that is wonderful for painting designs onto the surface of a cake.

Liquid colours

These are used to colour royal icing as they alter the consistency of flower-, sugar- and almond pastes but they can also be great to paint with. I use a small selection of liquid colours to paint fine spots and fine lines to petals.

Glazing

Glazing can give a leaf or petal a more realistic appearance. Don't glaze flowers too heavily as this can make them look unnatural. The methods described below are ways of glazing.

Steaming

Using powder colours on sugar flowers often leaves a dry looking finished flower – this can be changed to create a more waxy appearance and also help to set the colour to stop it leaving marks on the surface of the coated cake. Hold each flower in the steam from a boiling kettle for a few seconds, or until the surface turns slightly shiny. Take care not to get the sugar too wet as it will dissolve fairly fast. Allow the flower to dry before wiring into a spray. If you are creating a velvety finish to a rose for instance, then the steaming process can be used. You will then need to redust the flower. This technique will help an additional layer of dust to stick to the surface, giving the desired velvety effect.

Edible spray varnish

There are several ways to glaze leaves. Recently I have been using an edible spray varnish. This glaze can be used lightly for most leaves or sprayed in layers for shiny leaves and berries. You need to spray in a well-ventilated area and wear a filter mask.

Confectioners' varnish

Confectioners' varnish creates a wonderful glossy finish for berries and some leaves. However, I mostly dilute confectioners' varnish with isopropyl alcohol. Mix the two liquids together in a clean jam jar with a lid. Stir or swirl rather than shake the liquids to avoid producing air bubbles. Dip leaves into the glaze, shaking off the excess before hanging to dry or placing onto kitchen paper to blot off any excess. The glaze can also be painted onto the leaf but I find the bristles of the brush pull off some of the dust colour, producing a streaky effect. A build-up of glaze can give a very streaky, shiny finish. I use various strengths of glaze: three-quarter glaze (one part isopropyl alcohol to three parts confectioners' varnish) gives a high glaze but takes away the plastic finish often left by undiluted confectioners' varnish; half glaze (equal proportions of the two) gives a natural shine for many types of foliage; and quarter glaze (three parts isopropyl alcohol to one part confectioners' varnish) is used for leaves and petals that don't require a shine but just need something stronger than just steaming to set the colour and remove the dusty finish.

Recipes

Here are the basic recipes that you will need to make the projects in this book. There are recipes for icing, pastes and two different fruitcakes.

Flowerpaste

This type of paste is used to make fine sugar flowers. I usually buy ready-made flowerpaste (see Suppliers on page 143) as it tends to be more consistent, but the following is the recipe I use if I make my own.

INGREDIENTS
5 tsp cold water
2 tsp powdered gelatine
500 g (1 lb 2 oz/4½ cups) icing sugar, sifted
3 tsp gum tragacanth
2 tsp liquid glucose
4 tsp white vegetable fat
1 large free-range egg white

1 Mix the cold water and gelatine in a small bowl and leave to stand for 30 minutes. Sift the icing sugar and gum tragacanth together into the bowl of a heavy-duty mixer.

2 Place the bowl over a saucepan of hot water and stir until the gelatine has dissolved. Warm a teaspoon measure in hot water and measure out the liquid glucose – the heat of the spoon helps ease the glucose on its way. Add the glucose and 3 teaspoons of white fat to the gelatine mixture and continue to heat until all the ingredients have dissolved.

3 Add the dissolved mixture to the icing sugar with the egg white. Fit the beater to the machine and turn it on at its lowest speed. Gradually increase the speed to maximum until the paste is white and stringy.

4 Remove the paste from the bowl and knead. Cover the surface with the remaining teaspoon of white fat – this helps to prevent the formation of a dry crust that can leave hard bits in the paste when it is rolled out. Place in a plastic bag and store in an airtight container. Allow the paste to rest for 12 hours before using.

Royal icing

This recipe is ideal for the small amounts of royal icing required to create embroidery, lace, brush embroidery and other piped techniques.

INGREDIENTS
1 medium free-range egg white
  (at room temperature)
225 g (8 oz/2¼ cups) icing sugar, sifted

1 Wash the mixer bowl and the beater with a concentrated detergent, then scald to remove traces of grease and leftover detergent.

2 Place the egg white into the mixer bowl with most of the icing sugar and mix the two together with a spoon.

3 Fix the bowl and beater to the machine and beat on the slowest speed for about 8 minutes until the icing has reached full peak. You might need to add a little more icing sugar if the mixture is too soft.

Cold porcelain

This is an inedible air-drying craft paste that can be used in almost exactly the same way as flowerpaste. The advantage of this paste is that the flowers made from it are much stronger and less prone to breakages. The disadvantage is that because it is inedible the flowers need to be placed in a container to avoid direct contact with the cake's surface.

INGREDIENTS
2½ Tbsp baby oil
125 ml (4 fl oz/½ cup) non-toxic hi-tack glue (Impex)
125 ml (4 fl oz/½ cup) white PVA wood glue (Liberon super wood glue or Elmers)
125 g (4½ oz/1 cup) cornflour
Permanent white artists' gouache paint

1 Work in a well-ventilated area when making this paste. Wear a filter mask if you suffer from asthma. Place the baby oil and the two types of glue in a Teflon-coated saucepan and mix to form an emulsion. Stir the cornflour into the mixture – it will go lumpy but don't worry!

2 Place the pan over a medium heat and stir the paste with a heavy-duty plastic or wooden spoon. The paste will gradually come away from the base and the sides of the pan to form a ball around the spoon. Scrape any uncooked paste from the spoon and add to the mix. The cooking time will vary between gas, electric and ceramic hobs – the lower the heat and the slower you mix, the smoother the resulting paste will be. I'm impatient so I tend to turn the heat up a little to cook faster, about 10 minutes if that. Keep on stirring the paste to cook evenly. Split the paste and press the inner parts of the ball against the heat of the pan to cook it but be careful not to overcook as it will be impossible to work with. It is better if it is slightly undercooked as you can always add heat later.

3 Turn the paste onto a non-stick board and knead until smooth. The paste will be quite hot at this stage. The kneading should help distribute some heat through the paste to cook any undercooked areas. If the paste is very sticky you will need to put it back in the pan and cook it a little longer.

4 Wrap in clingfilm and leave to cool – moisture will build up on the surface of the paste so it is important to reknead it when cool and then rewrap it to avoid the growth of mould. Place in a plastic bag in an airtight container and store at room temperature. If stored correctly, this paste can keep for two years.

5 Prior to making flowers you will need to add a smidge of permanent white gouache paint. The paste looks white but by its nature dries clear, giving a translucence to the finished flower. Adding the paint makes the finish more opaque. Handling the paste is quite similar to working with flowerpaste except I use cold cream cleanser instead of white vegetable fat, and glue or anti-bacterial wipes/water to moisten the petals to stick them. Cornflour is used as for flowerpaste. The paste shrinks a little as it dries – this is because of the glue. This can be disconcerting to begin with but you get used to it and it can be an advantage when making miniature flowers.

Fruitcake

This is my favourite fruitcake – it is a variation of a recipe given to me by my friend Tombi Peck. Double the quantities for a three-tier wedding cake plus line another small tin just in case there is some left over. This recipe fills a 30-cm (12-in) square cake tin exactly (not that I ever make square cakes!) or a 30-cm (12-in) round cake tin, with a little left over for a smaller cake. The varieties and quantities of each dried fruit can be changed to suit your own taste.

INGREDIENTS

1 kg (2 lb 3 oz/6¾ cups) raisins
1 kg (2 lb 3 oz/6¾ cups) sultanas
500 g (1 lb 2 oz /3¼ cups) dried figs, chopped
500 g (1 lb 2 oz/3¼ cups) dried prunes, chopped
250 g (9 oz/2 cups) natural colour glacé cherries, halved
125 g (4½ oz/¾ cup) dried apricots, chopped
125 g (4½ oz/¾ cup) dried or glacé pineapple, chopped
Grated zest and juice of 1 orange
200 ml (7 fl oz/¾ cup) brandy (the odd dash of Cointreau or cherry brandy can be good too)
500 g (1 lb 2 oz/2 cups) unsalted butter, at room temperature
250 g (9 oz/1¼ cups) light muscovado sugar
250 g (9 oz/1¼ cups) dark muscovado sugar
20 ml (4 tsp) apricot jam
40 ml (8 tsp) golden syrup
5 ml (1 tsp) each of ground ginger, allspice, nutmeg, cloves and cinnamon
2.5 ml (½ tsp) ground mace
500 g (1 lb 2 oz/4 cups) plain flour
250 g (9 oz/2 cups) ground almonds
10 large free-range eggs, at room temperature

1 Halve and chop the various fruit that require it. Add or subtract the fruit accordingly to suit your taste but ensure the weight stays the same.

2 Mix the dried fruit, orange zest and juice, and alcohol together in a large plastic container with a lid. Seal and leave to soak for about a week if time allows. Otherwise overnight will do.

3 Cream the butter in a large bowl until soft. Gradually add the sugars and beat the two together. Stir in the apricot jam, golden syrup and spices.

4 Sieve the flour into a separate bowl and stir in the almonds. Beat the eggs together and add in batches to the butter/sugar mixture, alternating it with the flour/almond mix. Do not add the eggs too quickly as they might curdle.

5 Before you add the soaked fruit set aside a small amount of batter – this is used on top of the fruited batter to stop the fruit catching on the top in the oven. Mix the soaked fruit into the remaining larger amount of batter. Grease and line the tin(s) with non-stick parchment. Fill with batter to the required depth – aim for about two-thirds of the depth of the tin. Apply a thin layer of the unfruited batter on top and smooth over.

6 Bake at a very low heat – 140°C/ 275°F/gas 1 – for 4–6 hours, depending on the size of the cake. It is important to smell when the cake is ready as some ovens cook faster than others. The cake will shrink slightly from the side of the tin, be firm to the touch and smell wonderful. If in doubt test with a skewer – if it comes out clean the cake is ready.

7 Allow the cake to cool slightly in the tin, add a couple of extra dashes of alcohol and leave to cool further in the tin. Store wrapped in non-stick parchment and clingfilm. Allow the cake to mature for as long as you have – a few days up to a few months.

Sunshine fruitcake

This cake is a great option for those who find the more traditional fruitcake too heavy to appreciate. The original recipe was given to me by Pam Robinson from the Belfast branch of the British Sugarcraft Guild.

INGREDIENTS

150 g (5½ oz/1¼ cups) glacé cherries (multicoloured look great), halved and washed and allowed to dry (the addition of a small amount of chopped bright green angelica works wonders too, to give a jewelled finish)
100 g (3½ oz/1 cup) ground almonds
125 g (4½ oz/¾ cup) each of dried, ready-to-eat pineapple, mango, peach, apricot and pear, chopped
1 medium Bramley apple, grated
50 g (2 oz/2 squares) grated white chocolate
75 g (2½ oz/¾ cup) dried cranberries
3 Tbsp brandy (cherry brandy or Calvados work well too!), optional
225 g (8 oz/1 cup) unsalted butter, at room temperature
225 g (8 oz/1 cup) caster sugar
1 tsp salt
4 large free-range eggs
250 g (9 oz/2 cups) plain flour
1 level tsp baking powder
1 tsp vanilla essence

1 Preheat the oven to 180°C/350°F/ gas 4. Grease and line a 20-cm (8-in) round cake tin with non-stick parchment.

2 Toss the cherries in the ground almonds and set aside. Chop the remaining exotic fruits and then toss them with the diced apple, grated chocolate, cranberries and brandy and leave for an hour or so.

3 Beat the butter, sugar and salt together until pale and fluffy. Beat in the eggs one at a time, alternating with a tablespoon of flour and beating well between each addition. Stir in the remaining flour and vanilla essence and the baking powder. Then add the exotic fruit mixture and the cherries with the ground almonds and stir well to incorporate the fruit.

4 Spoon the mixture into the prepared cake tin and level the top. Bake for 30 minutes, then turn the heat down to 150°C/300°F/gas 2 and cook for a further 1½–2 hours. Cover the cake with foil or turn the oven down a little if you feel the top is catching.

5 Leave the cake to cool in the tin before turning out.

FLOWERS

Rose

Roses (Rosa) are the most requested flowers for bridal work and for cake decorators too! There are several methods for creating roses – the method described here is the style that I prefer and use most often.

MATERIALS

18-, 24-, 26-, 28- and 30-gauge white wires
Nile green floristry tape
White, pale vine green and holly/ivy flowerpaste
Fresh egg white
Daffodil, sunflower, edelweiss white, plum, forest green, foliage, vine green, moss and aubergine petal dusts
Cornflour
Half glaze or edible spray varnish (Fabilo)

EQUIPMENT

Fine-nose pliers
Rolling pin
Rose petal cutters (TT549, 550,551)
Foam pad
Metal ball tool (Cc)
Very large rose petal veiner (SKGI)
Dusting brushes
Cocktail stick, optional
Kitchen paper
Rose calyx cutter, optional
Sharp curved scissors
Set of three black rose leaf cutters (Jem)
Extra large rose leaf cutter (Jem)
Large briar rose leaf veiner (SKGI)
Smooth ceramic tool (HP)

ROSE CONE CENTRE

1 Tape over a half- to three-quarter length of 18-gauge white wire with half-width nile green floristry tape. Bend a large open hook in the end using fine-nose pliers. Form a ball of well-kneaded white flowerpaste into a cone shape to measure about two-thirds the length of the smallest rose petal cutter you are planning to use. Moisten the hook with fresh egg white and insert it into the rounded base of the cone. Push the hook into most of the length of the cone. Pinch the base of the paste onto the wire to secure the two together. Reshape the point of the cone if required – I tend to form a sharp point with a more rounded base. Allow to dry for as long as possible.

2 Colour a large amount of flowerpaste to the required colour; here I have used vine green petal dust to give a soft off-white base colour. I usually colour the paste paler than I want the finished rose to be.

FIRST AND SECOND LAYERS

3 Roll out some of the coloured paste fairly thinly. Cut out four petals using the smaller of the two rose petal cutters you are planning to use. Place the petals on a foam pad and soften the edges using a metal ball tool – work half on the edge of the petal and half on the pad using a rolling action with the tool. Try not to frill the edges at this stage as you are only taking away the raw cut edge of the petal. Vein each of the petals in turn using the double-sided rose petal veiner – dust with a little cornflour if needed to prevent sticking – especially if your veiner is being used for the first time. For smaller roses it is not always essential to vein the petals but the larger flowers benefit from it greatly.

4 Place the first petal against the dried cone using a little fresh egg white to help stick it in place. It needs to be positioned quite high against the cone so that you have enough of the petal to curl tightly to form a spiral effect around the cone. It is important that this cone is not visible

one of the petals slightly open to take the first petal of the next layer. Some roses have slightly pinched petals – this can be done as you add each layer by pinching the top edge to create a slight point. This number of petals can be used to make small rosebuds but the cone base should be made slightly smaller so that the petals cover the whole of it.

from the overview of the finished rose. Do not worry about covering the cone near the base – there are plenty more petals to follow that will do that job. I tend to curl the petal in from the left-hand side. Leave the right-hand edge of the petal slightly open so that the next petal can be tucked underneath it.

5 Moisten the remaining three petals and start the second layer by tucking a petal underneath the first petal on the cone. Stick down the edge of the first petal over the new petal. Place the next petal over the join created and then turn the rose to add the third petal. I tend to keep these petals open to start with so that I can get the positioning correct before tightening them around the cone to form a spiral shape. Leave

THIRD, FOURTH AND FIFTH LAYERS

6 Roll out some more coloured flowerpaste and cut out nine petals using the same size cutter as earlier. Soften the edges and vein the petals as before. Cover the petals with a plastic bag to stop them drying out – otherwise it is a case of cutting out and working on only three petals at a time. Tuck the first petal underneath the open petal from the previous layer of the rosebud and continue to add the other petals as described above, attaching them in

layers of three petals at a time. It is important to keep positioning petals over joins in the previous layer and not to line up petals directly behind each other. Gradually start to loosen the petals slightly as you work on the fourth and fifth layers. Pinch and curl the edges slightly more as you attach the fifth layer.

SIXTH LAYER

7 Roll out more coloured flowerpaste and cut out three petals using the slightly larger rose petal cutter. Soften and vein as before. This time start to hollow out the centre of each petal using a large ball tool or by simply rubbing the petal with your thumb.

8 Moisten the base of each petal creating a V shape. Attach to the rose as before, trying to place each petal over a join in the previous layer. Pinch either side of the petal at the base as you attach them so that it remains the cupped shape and allows the rose to breathe. Curl back the edges using a cocktail stick or just your fingers to create more movement in the petal edges. I tend to curl either edge of the petal, creating a more pointed petal shape. At this stage you have made what is termed a 'half rose'.

kitchen-paper ring former. Repeat to make about eight to ten petals. The number varies with each rose I make. As the petals are beginning to firm up you can keep going back to add extra curls to the edges if required.

ASSEMBLY AND COLOURING

10 I tape the individually wired petal around the half rose and then dust the rose as a whole – I find I balance the colour better this way. You might prefer to dust and then tape. It is best if the petals are not quite dry at this stage so that you can reshape and manipulate them to form a more pleasing rose shape. Tape the first wired petal over a join in the petals of the half rose using half-width nile green tape. The next petal is placed onto the opposite side of the rose. Continue adding the petals to cover gaps and joins in the previous layer. Remember not to place petals in line with petals of the layer underneath.

11 Mix together edelweiss white, vine green, daffodil and sunflower petal dusts. Probe the flower with a brush loaded with this mix to add a 'glow' at the base of each petal on the back and front. I tend to be heavier with this colour on the back of the petals. Next, decide which colours you are using to colour the bulk of the rose. The rose pictured has been dusted lightly with a very light mixture of vine green, moss and edelweiss petal dusts.

FINAL LAYER

9 I prefer to wire the petals individually for the final layer of the rose. This gives more movement and also a much stronger finished flower. Roll out some coloured flowerpaste, leaving a subtle ridge down the centre. Cut out the petal using the same size cutter as for the previous layer. Hook and moisten the end of a 26-gauge white wire. Insert it into the very base of the ridge. Soften the edges and vein as described previously. You will need to dust cornflour onto either the petal or the veiner at this stage to prevent them sticking together. Press the veiner firmly to create stronger veins. Remove from the veiner and hollow out the centre using your thumb and also start to curl back the edges. Allow the petal to dry slightly in a

FLOWERS

CALYX

12 As the outer petals of the rose have been individually wired I find it is best to wire each sepal of the calyx too. This gives a stronger finish but also allows the flower maker to represent a calyx with very long, slender sepals. A quicker calyx may be added using a rose calyx cutter if time won't allow a wired calyx. Cut five lengths of 28-gauge white wire. Work a ball of holly/ivy coloured flowerpaste onto the wire, creating a long, tapered carrot shape. Place the shape against the board and flatten using the flat side of one of the double-sided veiners. If the shape looks distorted, trim into shape with sharp scissors.

13 Place the flattened shape onto a foam pad or the palm of your hand, and soften and hollow out the length using the metal ball tool. Pinch the sepal from the base to the tip. Cut fine 'hairs' into the edge of the sepal using a pair of sharp curved scissors. Repeat to make five sepals. I tend to leave one sepal without hairs – although some varieties have no hairs to their calyces at all.

14 Dust each sepal on the outer surface with a mixture of foliage and forest green. Add tinges of aubergine mixed with plum or ruby petal dust. Use the same brush used for the green mixture and dust lightly on the inner surface of each sepal with white petal dust. Lightly glaze the back of each sepal with edible spray varnish.

15 Tape the five sepals to the base of the rose, positioning a sepal over a join. Add a ball of paste for the ovary and pinch and squeeze it into a neat shape. Dust and glaze to match the sepals.

LEAVES

16 I don't often use rose leaves as a foliage in bridal bouquets, however, they are essential for arrangements. Rose leaves on commercial florists' roses tend to grow in sets of three or five. I make one large, two medium and two small for each set. Roll out some holly/ivy flowerpaste, leaving a thick ridge for the wire – a grooved board can speed up this process. Cut out the leaves using the rose leaf cutters. The black rose leaf set does not allow for very thick leaves – these tend to stick in the cutter. Insert a moistened 26-, 28- or 30-gauge white wire, depending on its size, about half way into the ridge of the leaf.

17 Soften the edge of the leaf and vein using the large briar rose leaf veiner. Pinch from behind the leaf to accentuate the central vein and give more movement to the leaf. Repeat to make leaves of various sizes. Tape over a little of each wire stem with quarter-width nile green floristry tape. Tape the leaves into

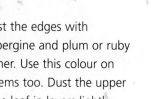

sets of three or five, starting with the largest leaf and two medium-size leaves, one on either side. Finally add the two smaller leaves at the base.

18 Dust the edges with aubergine and plum or ruby mixed together. Use this colour on the upper stems too. Dust the upper surface of the leaf in layers lightly with forest green and heavier with foliage and vine green. Dust the backs with white petal dust using the brush used for the greens. Spray with edible spray varnish.

Heart's desire orchid

I first saw these pretty orchids during a visit to an early-morning flower market in São Paulo, Brazil. At the time I was not sure what type of orchid it was and it was only after consulting several of my orchid books that I found that they are actually part of the Laelia orchid family, which is native to South America.

MATERIALS
White and green flowerpaste
22-, 24-, 26- and 28-gauge white wires
Plum, edelweiss white, African violet, aubergine, daffodil, foliage, forest and vine green petal dusts
White and nile green floristry tape
Edible spray varnish (Fabilo)
Cyclamen liquid colour (SKGI)

EQUIPMENT
Wire cutters
Smooth ceramic tool
Rolling pin
Non-stick board
Heart's desire orchid cutters (AD) or see templates on page 141
Sharp scalpel
Metal ball tool
Stargazer B petal veiner (SKGI)
Fine tweezers
Small ball tool
Dresden tool
Dusting brushes
Grooved board
Plain-edge cutting wheel (PME)
Large tulip leaf veiner (SKGI)

COLUMN

1 Form a small ball of well-kneaded white flowerpaste into a cone shape. Cut a short length of 26-gauge white wire, moisten and insert it into the fine end of the cone so that it supports most of the length. Line up the wired cone against the rounded end of a ceramic tool so that it is slightly higher than the tip. Press the paste against the tool to hollow out the underside of the column. Thin out the side edges slightly too. Leave to dry overnight if time allows.

LIP/LABELLUM

2 Roll out some white paste leaving a fine central ridge – this is not to be wired but gives extra support to the shape. Cut out the lip/labellum shape using either the cutter or the template on page 141 and a sharp scalpel. Soften the edge of the petal with the metal ball tool.

3 Vein using the double-sided stargazer B petal veiner. Use fine tweezers to pinch two small ridges at the base of the petal. Use a small ball tool to hollow out the two side sections of the petal.

4 Moisten the base and two bottom side edges of the column and position the hollowed side down against the lip/labellum. Carefully press the two side sections of the petal onto the column. Flick back the edges of these side sections and curl the tip of the lip too. You should have a gap between the lip petal and the underside of the column – if this is not the case then simply open up

the centre using the broad end of the dresden tool. Leave to firm up slightly before colouring.

5 Dust very gently with a light mixture of African violet, plum and edelweiss petal dusts. Increase the plum colouring at the tip of the lip. Add a dark patch of aubergine into the throat. Add a slight yellow tinge beyond the aubergine deep into the throat with a little daffodil petal dust. Paint a series of five lines over the dark dusted area using cyclamen liquid colour and a fine paintbrush.

LATERAL PETALS

6 Roll out some white paste leaving a fine ridge for the wire (you can use a grooved board for this). Cut out the petal shape using the widest of the three outer petals shapes. Insert a short length of moistened 28-gauge white wire into the thick ridge of the petal to support about half the length.

7 Soften the edge of the petal and then texture with the stargazer B petal veiner. Pinch the petal from the base to the tip to create a very gentle central vein and curve to the petal. Repeat to make two matching petals.

DORSAL AND LATERAL SEPALS

8 Repeat the process described in steps 6 and 7 to create the dorsal sepal using the longer of the two narrow cutters, and two lateral sepals using the shorter of the cutters or use the templates on page 141 and a sharp scalpel.

COLOURING AND ASSEMBLY

9 Gently dust the petals and outer sepals back and front, from both the base and the tip, with the light mixture of African violet, edelweiss and plum used earlier on the lip.

10 Using quarter-width white floristry tape, attach the two lateral petals onto either side of the lip/labellum. Next, position the dorsal sepal behind, covering the gap between the two petals. Tuck the two lateral sepals into the underside of the orchid and tape over the stem to create a neat finish. It helps at this stage if the petals/sepals are still pliable so that you can create a more realistic, relaxed flower shape.

11 Attach a ball of well-kneaded white paste onto the stem behind the flower and work it into a fine neck shape. Blend the join between the ball of paste and the petals using the broad end of the dresden tool. Curve the stem slightly and dust with the flower colour plus a tinge of vine green and white from the base of the neck.

BUDS

12 Cut lengths of 26-gauge white wire into thirds. Form a ball of well-kneaded white paste into a cone shape and insert the wire into the broad end of the cone. Work the paste down the stem to create the long neck shape of the flower.

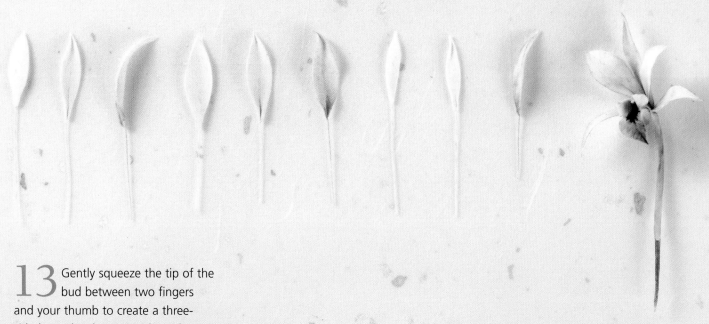

13 Gently squeeze the tip of the bud between two fingers and your thumb to create a three-sided angular shape. Divide each side with the plain-edge cutting wheel – this represents the three outer sepals of the flower. Curve the neck gently. Repeat to make several buds in graduating sizes. Dust as for the flower.

LEAVES

14 Roll out some green paste leaving a long thick ridge for the wire. Cut out the long narrow straplike leaf using the plain-edge cutting wheel. Insert a 22- or 24-gauge wire into the thick ridge to support at least half the length of the leaf.

15 Texture using the large tulip leaf veiner. Remove from the veiner and pinch from the base to the tip to accentuate the central vein and give it a graceful curve. Allow to firm up a little before dusting.

16 Dust in layers with forest, foliage and vine green. Add a tinge of aubergine to the tip and the base. Leave to dry and then spray lightly with edible spray varnish or dip into a half glaze.

ASSEMBLY AND PSEUDO-BULB

17 Tape a group of buds onto the end of a 22-gauge wire using nile green floristry tape. Introduce one or two flowers and tape tightly.

18 The leaves and flowers of the plant grow from a pseudo-bulb. This is not essential to make but can be quite fun to incorporate. Tape one or two leaves at the base of the flower stem and then add a ball of green paste. Blend the ball into a slight point at both ends and pinch and flatten the sides.

19 Use the plain-edge cutting wheel to draw a series of lines over the surface of the bulb. Dust as for the leaves and varnish or glaze.

Christmas orchid

This is a terrestrial orchid that was prized by the Victorians and nicknamed the 'Christmas orchid' as it flowers profusely during that period. It actually flowers from the autumn through to February. Its Latin name, Calanthe, translated means 'with lovely flowers'. There are pure white, pink, red and burgundy forms.

MATERIALS
White and pale green flowerpaste
22-, 26-, 28-, 30, 33- and 35-gauge
  white wires
Plum, vine, foliage and aubergine petal
  dusts
Nile green floristry tape

EQUIPMENT
Rolling pin
Non-stick board
Simple leaf cutters (TT229, 230)
Wire cutters
Sharp fine scissors
Silk veining tool (HP)
Sharp scalpel
Cupped Christmas rose petal veiner (SKGI)

LIP/LABELLUM

1 Roll out some well-kneaded white flowerpaste leaving a thick ridge for the wire. Cut out the lip shape using one of the two sizes of simple leaf cutter. Cut a length of 26-gauge wire into thirds. Moisten the end of one of the wires and insert into the pointed end of the petal. Work the base of the petal down onto the wire to elongate the shape slightly.

2 Use sharp fine scissors to alter the shape of the petal, cutting out one V-shaped cut at the top of the lip and one either side of the lip.

3 Broaden, vein and slightly frill each section of the lip using the silk veining tool. Rest the petal against your finger or on the board while the tool is being rolled against the petal.

4 Open up the base of the petal to create an opening that will form the column of the flower. Pinch the petal from the base to the tip to create a central vein and curve it slightly. Leave to set a little before the next stage.

5 Attach a small ball of paste just above the hollowed-out area of the lip. This represents the anther cap. Divide the cap into two sections using a sharp scalpel.

COLOURING

6 Dust the petal with plum petal dust. In this example I have faded the colour towards the edges of the petal but some of the Christmas orchids have a very intense pink, red or burgundy lip. Add a tinge of aubergine into the throat of the orchid.

LATERAL (WING) PETALS

7 I find these petals easier to make using a freehand technique. Cut short lengths of 30-gauge white wires. Roll a ball of white well-kneaded flowerpaste and then form into a cone shape. Insert a wire into the broad end of the cone. Work the base of the cone down onto the wire to create an elongated petal shape.

8 Place the wired shape against a non-stick board and 'flatten the petal using the flat side of the Christmas rose petal veiner. You might need to trim the thinned petal into shape but with practice you will create a more consistent petal shape.

9 Soften the edge of the petal and then vein using the cupped Christmas rose veiner. Pinch the petal to create a central vein. Repeat to make two lateral petals.

DORSAL AND LATERAL SEPALS

10 Repeat the above process to create a dorsal and two lateral sepals – you should aim to make these a little narrower in shape.

NECTARY/SPUR

11 There is a very fine nectary that follows through from the column and the lip. It is easiest to make this as a separate wired piece. Use a short length of 33- or 35-gauge white wire and roll a tiny ball onto the end. Work the paste down the wire to create a fine coating. The length of the nectary varies between different varieties of Christmas orchids – just make sure that you are fairly consistent with the length you create if making a lot of these orchids for a cake. Curve the nectary and then tape onto the base of the lip so that it curves below it.

ASSEMBLY

12 Use half-width nile green floristry tape to attach the two lateral petals onto either side of the lip. Position the dorsal sepal behind the petals to fill the gap and the two lateral sepals at the base of the flower. Encourage them all to fall away from the lip.

BUDS

13 Cut a length of 28-gauge wire into thirds. Roll a ball of white flowerpaste and form it into a cone shape. Work the base of the cone to create the long fine nectary/spur shape. Bend a hook in the end of a length of 28-gauge wire and insert into the centre of the bud. Pinch into place and then create a three-sided angular effect to the broader end by simply pressing it between two fingers and a thumb.

14 Divide the top section into three to represent the three outer sepals. Curve the nectary to the underside of the bud.

BRACTS

15 These are made in the same way as the outer petals of the orchid but use finer wire for the smaller bracts and pale green paste. Make one bract for each flower and bud, plus a few extras for the top of the stem. Dust lightly with vine green and foliage petal dust.

FINAL ASSEMBLY

16 Start by snuggling a few of the tiny green bracts at the end of a 22-gauge wire. Tape them into place using half-width nile green tape. Gradually introduce a small bud accompanied by a leaf and continue down the stem, increasing the size of the buds and bracts until you are ready to introduce a flower and a bract. Bend the stem into a graceful curve. Dust the stem with foliage and vine green. Add tinges of aubergine to the tips of the bracts if desired.

Begonia

There are over 900 species of begonia widely distributed throughout the tropics and subtropics but particularly in South America. It is the ornate leaves of Begonia rex that I like the most. They are great for filling spaces in a bouquet or arrangement, while providing interesting colour and texture.

MATERIALS
Pale green flowerpaste
20-, 22- and 24-gauge white wires
Aubergine, foliage, plum and African
   violet petal dusts
Isopropyl alcohol
Nile green floristry tape
Myrtle bridal satin dust (optional)
Edible spray varnish (Fabilo)

EQUIPMENT
Rolling pin
Non-stick board
Begonia leaf cutters (AD) or see
   templates on page 140
Sharp scalpel (optional)
Begonia leaf veiners (SKGI and Aldaval)
Dresden tool (J)
Dimpled foam (or similar)
No. 2 paintbrush
Dusting brushes

LEAVES

1 The paste needs to be rolled quite thickly for these leaves as the veiners have short, deep veining to them. You will find that at times they get hungry and bite into the paste – you can sort this out by overlapping the tear and persuading the leaf to mend itself. Roll out the paste leaving a thicker ridge for the wire. Cut out the leaf using a begonia leaf cutter or the templates on page 140 and a sharp scalpel.

2 Insert a moistened wire heavy enough to support the size of leaf you are working on. Place the leaf into the veiner so that the wire runs in line with the central vein on the back of the leaf. Squeeze the two sides of the veiner together to sandwich the leaf. Remove from the veiner and pinch the central and side veins to accentuate them and give them more movement. Turn the leaf over and use the broad end of the dresden tool to create a rough, slightly ragged, frilled edge. Allow the leaf to dry over dimpled foam or similar.

COLOURING

3 It is best to have a picture or a real leaf to copy when painting designs on the surface. Dilute some aubergine or foliage green petal dust (I used aubergine) with isopropyl alcohol. Paint in the main lines radiating from the base of the leaf with a no. 2 paintbrush. Add a border of colouring around the edge of the leaf too. Allow the lines to dry.

4 Dust the back of the leaf heavily with a mixture of plum and African violet petal dusts. Add a little of this colour to the upper surface of the leaf. Next, use some foliage green or aubergine, or both, from the edge of the leaf to the centre. If the painted lines look a little scary simply dust some foliage or aubergine over the lines to soften them. Thicken the stem with a few layers of nile green floristry tape and dust to match the leaf.

5 Add a light dusting of myrtle bridal satin dust or similar if you are making a shiny variety of begonia. Spray lightly with edible spray varnish.

Hosta

Loved by slugs and snails everywhere, these wonderful leaves are also favoured by florists and flower arrangers. There are many variegated forms as well as albino forms but it is the plainer forms that I prefer.

MATERIALS
Pale or mid-green flowerpaste
20- or 22-gauge white wire
Forest, foliage, edelweiss and aubergine
 petal dusts
Edible spray varnish (Fabilo)

EQUIPMENT
Rolling pin
Non-stick board
Hosta leaf templates, see page 141
Sharp scalpel or plain-edge cutting
 wheel (PME)
Hosta leaf veiners (SKGI or Aldaval)
Foam pad
Large ball tool
Dusting brushes

LEAVES

1 Roll out the paste so that it is quite fleshy, leaving a thicker ridge for the wire. Cut out the leaf shape using the templates on page 141 and a sharp scalpel or plain-edge cutting wheel.

2 Insert a moistened wire into the thick ridge of the leaf so that it is supported by at least half the length of the wire. Place the leaf onto a foam pad or in your palm if it is big enough and soften the edge using a large ball tool. Vein using the double-sided hosta leaf veiner.

3 Pinch the leaf from the base through to the tip to accentuate the central vein. Dry curved or flatter, depending on how you intend to use it in the spray or arrangement. Allow to settle a little before dusting.

COLOURING

4 Dust in light layers with forest and then a heavier mixture of foliage and edelweiss petal dusts – a larger brush will be needed for larger leaves. The back should be pale. Catch the edges and the base of the leaf lightly with aubergine – this will depend upon the depth of colour and variety you are making. Allow to dry and then spray lightly with edible spray varnish.

Orchid tree

Known as the orchid tree because of its almost exotic orchid-like flowers, it is from the Bauhinia family. There are about 200 species of Bauhinia so there is lots of room for interpretation. The flowers shown here are fairly small but many of the Bauhinias can be quite large. There are five petals to each flower, I often refer to them as the head, arms and legs! There are three cutters in the Bauhinia cutters set.

MATERIALS
White and pale green flowerpaste
24-, 26-, 28-, 30- and 33-gauge white wires
African violet, plum, edelweiss, sunflower, primrose, vine, foliage and aubergine petal dusts
Nile green floristry tape
Cyclamen liquid colour
Half glaze or edible spray varnish (Fabilo)

EQUIPMENT
Wire cutters
Dusting brushes
Rolling pin
Non-stick board
Grooved board (optional)
Bauhinia petal cutters (TT463-465) or for a larger flower (TT 460-462) or see the templates on page 140
Medium metal ball tool
Bauhinia petal veiners or rose petal veiner (SKGI)
Fine paintbrush
Plain-edge angled tweezers
Fine-nose pliers
Bauhinia leaf cutters (AD)
Bauhinia leaf veiners (SKGI)

PISTIL

1 The Bauhinia belongs to the pea family and its pistil resembles that of most of the pea family. Work a small ball of pale green flowerpaste onto a short length of 33-gauge white wire. Try to make the tip finer by working the paste firmly between your finger and thumb. Flatten the length of the pistil and then give it a graceful curve.

2 Dust lightly with vine green and edelweiss petal dusts. Add a darker tinge of aubergine if desired.

STAMENS

3 There are five stamens to the flower. Cut five short lengths of 33-gauge white wire. Work a tiny amount of white flowerpaste onto each, trying to keep the tip fine. Curve each stamen and allow to dry.

4 Attach a tiny sausage of white flowerpaste onto the tip of each stamen: this will represent the anther. Allow to set and then dust with a light mixture of sunflower, primrose and edelweiss petal dusts. Add a tinge of African violet/plum/edelweiss to each stamen.

5 Tape the five stamens onto the pistil. Bear in mind that the central stamen is longer than the others, the next two are slightly shorter and the remaining two are shorter again.

HEAD PETAL (DORSAL)

6 Roll out some white flowerpaste, leaving a thick ridge for the wire (a grooved board may help to speed up the flower-making process). Cut out the head petal shape using the appropriate cutter or the templates on page 140.

7 Insert a moistened 30-gauge wire into the base of the petal so that it supports about a third to half the length of the shape. Soften the edges of the petal with a medium ball tool.

8 Vein using the single-sided Bauhinia veiner or double-sided rose petal veiner. Pinch the length of the shape to accentuate the central vein. Curl back slightly and allow to firm up.

ARM AND LEG PETALS (LATERAL PETALS)

9 These are made as above but you need to flip the cutters over to create a left and right arm and leg combination. Soften and vein as above. Curve all the petals back and allow to firm up before assembling and colouring.

ASSEMBLY

10 You might prefer to colour the flower and then assemble. I prefer to create the complete flower shape and then dust the colour as I find a more balanced result is achieved. Tape the head petal onto the stamens using quarter-width nile green floristry tape so that they curl towards the petal. Next add the arms tucked slightly behind the head petal and finally the legs. If the paste is still pliable at this stage it will help you to create a more realistic shape.

COLOURING

11 Dust the petals from the edge using a light mixture of plum, African violet and edelweiss petal dusts. Add a light patch of sunflower, primrose and edelweiss to the heart of the head petal.

12 Paint a series of fine lines onto the head petal using a very fine paintbrush and the cyclamen liquid colour. Allow the flower to dry and then steam gently to set the colour on the flower.

BRACTS

13 There is a bract behind each flower. The style of bract varies between the 200 species! Roll out some pale green paste and cut out a pointed arrowhead shape. Soften the edges and then pinch a series of lines down the length using plain-edge angled tweezers.

14 Moisten the wire behind the flower and attach the bract behind, wrapping it around the wire to secure it in place. Dust lightly with vine green and foliage petal dusts. Catch the edge gently with aubergine.

BUDS

15 Cut short lengths of 28-gauge wire. Bend a hook in the end of each. Form a ball of pale green paste into a slender cone shape. Insert a moistened hooked wire into the broad end. Work the base of the cone down onto the wire. Mark a single deep line down one side of the bud – this represents the bract shrouding the petals beneath. Dust as for the bract.

LEAVES

16 Roll out some green paste leaving a thick ridge for a wire. Cut out the leaf using one of the Bauhinia leaf cutters. Insert a 28-, 26- or 24-gauge wire (depending upon the size of the leaf you are making) into the ridge.

17 Soften the edge gently and then texture using a Bauhinia leaf veiner. Pinch to accentuate the central vein. Allow to firm up slightly before dusting.

18 Dust the edges with aubergine petal dust. Dust foliage and then vine onto the upper surface and add a paler dusting to the back of the leaf. Dip into a half glaze or spray very lightly with edible spray varnish.

Hoya

The fine terete foliage of Hoya teretifolia *can be very effective in bridal bouquets to trail, create length and at the same time it has a wonderful softening quality.*

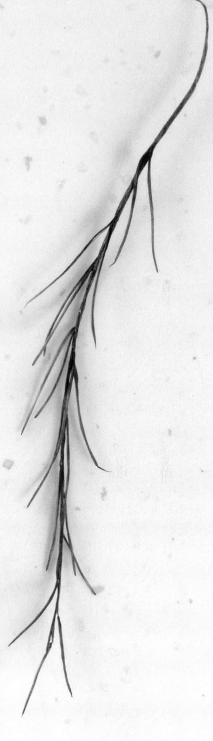

MATERIALS
28-, 30- and 33-gauge white wires
Pale green flowerpaste
Nile green floristry tape
Foliage, edelweiss and aubergine petal
    dusts
Edible spray varnish (Fabilo)

EQUIPMENT
Wire cutters
Non-stick board
Plain-edge cutting wheel
Dusting brushes
Fine-nose pliers

LEAVES

1 Cut short lengths of 33- or 30-gauge white wires.

2 Attach a small ball of pale green paste onto a wire, blending it to form a long, slender terete leaf. Smooth the leaf against the non-stick board or between your palms. Use the plain-edge cutting wheel to mark a central vein. Repeat to create leaves in pairs, increasing in size.

ASSEMBLY

3 Tape two tiny leaves onto the end of a 28-gauge wire using quarter-width nile green floristry tape. Leave a space on the main stem and then add another pair of leaves. Continue adding the leaves, graduating the size as you work down the stem. Fine-nose pliers will help you to position the leaves neatly in place.

4 Dust the leaves with a mixture of foliage and edelweiss petal dusts. Add tinges of aubergine. Spray lightly with edible spray varnish.

Spider chrysanthemum

Chrysanthemum are cultivated and grown the world over and have become very popular as cut flowers. This form of chrysanthemum originates from the Orient. These are very effective flowers to make in sugar or cold porcelain, but they are really very time-consuming. It is best to build up the many petals over a period of days rather than trying to complete the flower in a day.

MATERIALS
Pale vine green and mid-green flowerpaste
35-, 33-, 30-, 28-, 26- and 22-gauge
    white wires
Vine green, moss, forest, foliage and
    aubergine petal dusts
Nile green floristry tape
Edible spray varnish (Fabilo)

EQUIPMENT
Fine-nose pliers
Sharp scalpel or plain-edge cutting wheel
Smooth ceramic tool or paintbrush
Fine curved scissors
Dusting brushes
Wire cutters
Cocktail sticks or fine celstick
Daisy cutters in assorted sizes
Rolling pin
Non-stick board
Chrysanthemum leaf cutter (Jem)
Chrysanthemum leaf veiner (SKGI)

CENTRE

1 Roll a ball of well-kneaded pale vine green flowerpaste. Bend an open hook in the end of a 22-gauge wire using fine-nose pliers. Moisten the hook and pull it through the ball of paste. Blend the ball and pinch it onto the wire to secure it in place.

2 Texture the surface of the ball using a sharp scalpel or plain-edge cutting wheel to mark a series of fine lines radiating from the centre to represent the inner petals. Indent the centre slightly using the rounded end of the ceramic tool or a paintbrush handle.

3 Use a pair of fine curved scissors to snip at the indented section of the centre and also to snip some petals around the edge of the ball. Leave to dry overnight.

4 Dust with vine green and a little moss green petal dust.

OUTER PETALS

5 Cut lengths of 35-, 33-, 30- or 28-gauge wire, depending on the size of petals you are working on. This is not an exercise of exact numbers. You simply keep making and taping the petals around the centre, starting with very fine petals and gradually increasing them in size. It is best to tape the petals onto the centre while they are still wet so that you can reshape to create a more realistic flower shape. Work a small ball of paste onto each wire working the paste towards the tip. Smooth down the sides between the fleshy part of your hands.

6 Hollow out the tip using a cocktail stick, fine celstick or the point of the ceramic tool. Curve the length of the petal prior to taping onto the dried centre with quarter- or half-width nile green floristry tape. Once you have several petals around the centre you can start to reshape

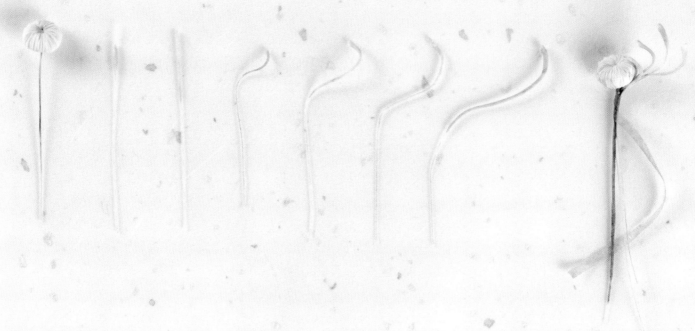

them. Continue making and adding petals, gradually increasing in size as you build up each layer.

7 Dust with vine green and touches of moss green. Spray lightly with edible spray varnish or steam to set the colour and give a gentle shine.

CALYX

8 I am tempted to omit the calyx if the flower is to be displayed in a tight arrangement or spray. However, if you are creating a flower for a competition or an arrangement where the back will be visible it is best to add a calyx. Use a few layers of shapes cut out using a daisy cutter or attach lots of individual fine green sepals to the back of the flower. Dust with foliage green.

LEAVES

9 Roll out some mid-green flowerpaste leaving a thick ridge for the wire. Cut out the leaf shape using a chrysanthemum leaf cutter. Insert a 26-gauge wire into the thick ridge so that it supports about half the length of the leaf.

10 Soften the edges of the leaf and then texture using the chrysanthemum leaf veiner. Pinch the leaf to accentuate the central vein.

11 Hollow out the back of the leaf slightly and then allow to dry a little before dusting. Dust in layers with forest, foliage and very lightly with aubergine. The backs of the leaves are much paler than the upper surface. Spray lightly with edible spray varnish or steam to set the colour. Chrysanthemum leaves are generally not shiny, however sometimes sugar leaves need a tad of artistic licence.

Pitcher plant

Pitcher plants (Sarracenia) are native to North America and East Asia. They provide the flower arranger and the flower maker with an unusual form that adds immediate height and interest to an arrangement.

MATERIALS
20-, 22-, 24- and 26-
    gauge white wires
White floristry tape
Pale green flowerpaste
Vine, white, moss, foliage,
    forest, plum and
    aubergine petal dusts
Cyclamen liquid colour (SK)
Edible spray varnish

EQUIPMENT
Rolling pin
Non-stick board
Pitcher plant cutter (AD) or see the
    templates on page 142
Sharp scalpel (optional)
Hydrangea petal veiner (SKGI)
Ceramic silk veining tool
Medium or large ball tool
Fine scissors
Dusting brushes
Fine paintbrush

STRUCTURE AND CUTTING

1 Tape a 26-gauge wire onto a 24-, 22- or 20-gauge wire (depending upon the size of pitcher you are making) using half-width white floristry tape. Leave a little of the finer wire standing proud at the end of the stronger one – this will help to add support to the finer upper section of the pitcher.

2 Roll out some pale green flowerpaste, leaving a very long ridge running down the centre. The paste needs to be large enough to take the cutter shape and allow a little extra at the top to fold back over to sandwich the finer of the two wires.

3 Moisten the wire and press it into the ridged area of the paste. Pull the paste at the top over the finer wire to sandwich it. Reroll this section of the paste to thin it slightly and secure the wire inside. Cut out the shape using one of the three sizes of pitcher plant cutter or use a sharp scalpel and the templates on page 142.

4 Vein the top flap section using the hydrangea petal veiner so that the upper surface ends up with the ridges of the back of the hydrangea petal. Frill the frills slightly using silk veining tool.

5 Soften the edges of the shape using a medium or large ball tool. Turn back the top edges to create a fine collar and then moisten the length and pinch the two long side edges together. This will create a ridge-like seam that can be trimmed back slightly with fine scissors.

6 Pinch the top flap section at the tip and then persuade the bottom part of this to turn back slightly at the base. Curve the length.

COLOURING

7 Dust in layers with vine green mixed with a little white; then with moss, a touch of forest and foliage green. Use plum and aubergine to add depth to the ridged areas and the edges of the top flap section. Add a series of fine lines to the flap using a fine brush and cyclamen liquid colour. Spray lightly with edible spray varnish.

Poppy seed-head

Poppy seed-heads are great fun to make and add an interesting texture to arrangements and bouquets. Here the seed-heads are represented in a fairly fresh form but they look good created as dried seed-heads altering the colours to grey and brown.

MATERIALS
20- or 22-gauge white wires
Pale green flowerpaste
Fresh egg white
Forest, foliage, edelweiss and aubergine petal dusts
Nile green floristry tape

EQUIPMENT
Fine-nose pliers
Cocktail stick
Smooth ceramic tool
Rolling pin
Non-stick board
Small daisy cutter
Sharp scalpel
Plain-edge angled tweezers
Dust brushes

PREPARATION AND ASSEMBLY

1 Bend a hook in the end of a 20- or 22-gauge wire (depending upon how large you intend the pod to be). Form a ball of well-kneaded green paste into a barrel shape. Moisten the hooked wire and push into the paste. Reshape the sides and taper the tip of the pod slightly.

2 Pinch the base of the pod down onto the wire and mark with a cocktail stick to form a ridged area. Use the smooth ceramic tool to create a series of subtle lines down the sides of the pod.

3 Roll out some green paste quite thickly and cut out a daisy shape. Split each section in half using a sharp scalpel and part the sections slightly as you work.

4 Pinch a ridge down the length of each section using plain-edge angled tweezers. Moisten the tip of the pod with fresh egg white and position the daisy shape on top. Allow to dry slightly before dusting.

COLOURING

5 Dust with a mixture of forest, foliage and edelweiss petal dusts. Add tinges of aubergine if desired. Use the flat of the brush to catch the ridges on the daisy shape with aubergine too. Steam to set the colour.

6 Tape over the stem with half-width nile green floristry tape. Dust as for the seedhead.

Lily of the valley

I love making lily of the valley (Convallaria). This design was developed by my friend, Tombi Peck. She based the idea on one of Fabergé's Pearl lily of the valley designs. It is 20 years since she first showed me this flower but I have never tired of it.

MATERIALS
24- and 35-gauge white wires
White flowerpaste
Nile green floristry tape
Vine green and foliage petal dusts

EQUIPMENT
Wire cutters
Fine-nose pliers
Rolling pin
Non-stick board
Tiny five-petal plunger blossom cutter
  (PME)
Smooth ceramic tool (HP)
Dusting brush

BUDS

1 Cut several short lengths of 35-gauge white wire – you will need a lot of wire for the flowers and buds. Bend a hook in the end of each length of wire using fine-nose pliers. Roll lots of balls of white flowerpaste in graduating sizes. Insert a hooked wire into each and reshape if needed.

FLOWERS

2 Roll out a small amount of white flowerpaste and cut out a flower shape using the blossom cutter. Next, roll a ball of white paste and place the blossom shape onto the ball – if both pieces of paste are still fresh they will stick together without the need for fresh egg white.

3 Embed the blossom into the ball of paste using the pointed end of the ceramic tool, which should also help to create a hollowed out finish.

4 Moisten a hooked wire and thread it through the centre of the flower. Repeat to make five–seven flowers for each stem. Leave to dry.

ASSEMBLY AND COLOURING

5 Tape a tiny bud onto the end of a 24-gauge wire using quarter-width nile green floristry tape. Continue to add the buds, graduating the size as you add them to the stem. I usually use between five–nine buds per stem and then add between three and seven flowers.

6 Using fine-nose pliers curl the stem of each flower and bud so that their heads curve downwards.

7 Dust the main stem and each of the shorter ones with vine green petal dust. Add some of the colour to the smaller buds, gradually decreasing as you approach the flowers. Tinge the base of the main stem with foliage green petal dust.

Stephanotis

Sometimes known as the Madagascan jasmine, which is where the plant originates. Stephanotis floribunda is highly scented, and in the language of flowers, it is supposed to represent happiness in marriage, making it an ideal flower for bridal work!

MATERIALS
White and pale green flowerpaste
24- and 26-gauge white wires
Vine, daffodil, foliage and edelweiss petal dusts
Edible spray varnish

EQUIPMENT
Non-stick board
Smooth ceramic tool (HP)
Extra large stephanotis cutter (TT) or Nasturtium calyx cutter (TT448)
Dresden tool (J)
Flat dusting brushes
Small stephanotis cutter (TT568)
Sharp scalpel

FLOWERS

1 Form a ball of white paste into a sausage shape and pinch out one end to form a pedestal. Place the flat section against the board and roll out the base using the ceramic tool. Lift the shape up and place this rolled-out section on top of the extra large stephanotis or nasturtium calyx cutter.

2 Use the ceramic tool to roll over the paste against the edge of the cutter to cut out the shape. Rub your thumb over the edges to remove any fuzzy bits. Remove the shape from the cutter and place the flat part back against the board. Use the ceramic tool to broaden and elongate each of the petals slightly.

3 Open up the centre of the flower using the pointed end of the ceramic tool. Rest the flower against a finger and hollow out the centre of each petal using the broad end of the dresden tool.

4 Bend a hook in the end of a 24-gauge wire and pull through the centre of the flower. Work the back of the flower between your finger and thumb to create an arched slender back that broadens towards the base. Pinch off any excess paste at the base.

5 Dust the base with a light mixture of vine, daffodil and edelweiss petal dust. Add a tinge of colour at the flower centre too.

6 Roll out some pale green paste and cut out a calyx using the smallest stephanotis cutter. Soften the edges and attach to the base of the flower. Keep this shape fairly flat. Dust with vine and foliage green. Spray very lightly with edible spray varnish or steam to create a waxy finish.

BUDS

7 Hook and moisten a 24- or 26-gauge white wire depending upon the size of bud you are making. Form a cone shape of paste and insert the wire into the broad base. Work the paste as for the back of the flower to create its characteristic long neck. Divide the tip into five sections with a sharp scalpel. Twist very slightly if desired. Add a calyx as for the flower.

Gardenia

There are about 250 species of gardenia! The flowers are mostly white and cream but there are yellow and orange forms too. They are native to tropical and subtropical regions of Africa, Asia, Australasia and Oceania. Gardenias are used for button-holes, corsages and bridal bouquets, favoured because of their exquisite but heady scent.

MATERIALS

White and mid-green flowerpaste

22-, 24-, 26-, 28-, 30-, 33 and 35-gauge white wires

Vine, moss, forest, foliage, edelweiss and sunflower petal dusts

Nile green and white floristry tape

White seed-head stamens

Non-toxic hi-tack craft glue (Impex)

Clear alcohol

Three-quarter glaze or edible spray varnish (Fabilo)

EQUIPMENT

Fine-nose pliers

Flat-edge tweezers

Dusting brushes

Wire cutters

Cupped Christmas rose veiner (SKGI) or anemone petal veiner (ALDV)

Rolling pin

Non-stick board

Christmas rose (TT282, 283, 284) or Australian rose cutters (TT349-352) or gardenia cutters (AD) or see the Australian rose templates on page 141

Sharp scalpel

Foam pad

Dresden tool

Grooved board

Plain-edge cutting wheel (PME)

Ball tool

Gardenia leaf veiner (SKGI)

BUDS

1 Form a ball of well-kneaded white flowerpaste into a cone shape and insert a moistened, hooked 24- or 22-gauge wire into it. (The size of the wire will depend upon how big the bud is.) Work the base of the cone down onto the wire to create a slender neck.

2 Using flat-edge tweezers pinch six flange-like petals from around the upper section of the bud. Go back and thin the edges with your finger and thumb. Next, hold the petals and persuade them to spiral – the direction will depend upon the exact variety but try to make sure that the buds and flowers follow the same direction.

3 Dust with vine green and edelweiss petal dust – try to get some colour into the grooves of the petals.

CALYX

4 Cut six short lengths of 35- or 33-gauge wire. Attach a tiny ball of green paste to a wire and work it to blend a long slender sepal shape. Flatten the shape using the smooth side of a petal veiner. Pinch a ridge down the length between your finger and thumb and then curve slightly towards the tip. Repeat to make six sepals. Dust with foliage green petal dust.

5 Tape the six sepals around the base of the bud using half-width nile green floristry tape.

TIGHT CENTRE

6 You now need to decide if you are going to make a gardenia with a tight, spiralled centre or one that has matured to open up and reveal its centre. I have included instructions for both (see below). Bend a hook in the end of a 24-gauge wire using fine-nose pliers. Form a small cone shape of white paste and insert the moistened, hooked wire into the base. Leave to dry.

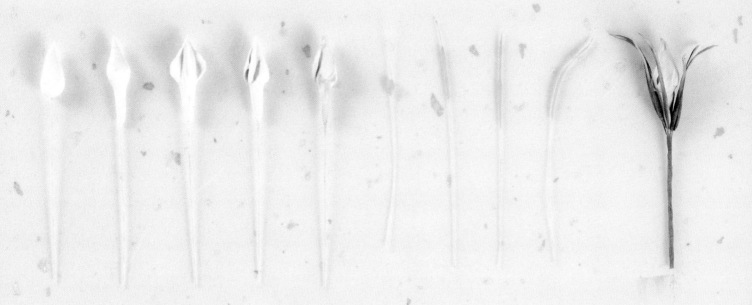

7 Roll out some white paste and cut out six small petals using your chosen style of petal cutter or use the gardenia petal templates on page 141. Soften the edges of the petals and then texture using the cupped Christmas rose (as used here) or the anemone petal veiner – which will create heavier veining.

8 Place the petals onto a foam pad and work on the inside edge on the left-hand side of each petal using the broad end of the dresden tool to encourage the petal to curl.

9 Moisten the dried cone or the petals with egg white and place the petals one by one onto the centre. Overlap them and tuck the last petal in to create a tight spiral. Curl back the edges if required.

OPEN CENTRE

10 Here are the instructions for the centre of a more mature flower. Use a 26-gauge wire to create the pistil. Blend a tiny amount of pale green paste onto the end to form a slender bud shape. Pinch a few ridges and then spiral the tip. Allow to dry.

11 Tape six seed-head stamen tips around the pistil using quarter-width nile green tape or simply attach them using hi-tack craft glue. Dust the tips with sunflower petal dust. Sometimes the stamens are more creamy in colour and as the flower fades they turn a more brown/aubergine colour.

12 Create six wired petals using the small cutter used for the tight centre method above. Roll out the paste to leave a thick ridge for a fine wire and then cut out the petal shape. Insert a moistened short length of 30-gauge wire into the ridge. Pinch the base of the petal down onto the wire to secure it in place. Soften the edges and vein as above. You may also want to create the curled edge as above too – this very much depends upon the style of gardenia you are making. Cup the centre very slightly. Repeat to make six petals.

13 Tape the six petals in a spiral form around the stamens using quarter-width white floristry tape.

15 Tape the outer petals onto the tight spiralled or more open centre using half-width white floristry tape. Try to position petals in between joins in the previous layer. Repeat to add the six larger petals. It helps if the petals are still pliable so that you can reshape and form a more interesting finish.

16 Add a ball of white paste to the back of the flower and work it down the wire to form a slender neck. Some gardenias have very long necks while others are fairly short. Blend the paste into the base of the petals using the broad end of the dresden tool and a touch of clear alcohol – try not to get the petals too wet as they will dissolve. Create and add six sepals as for the bud and tape to the base of the flower with half-width nile green tape.

COLOURING

17 Mix together vine green and edelweiss petal dusts. Add strong green colouring to the slender neck and under the curl of each of the outer petals. A little of the soft colour can be used at the centre of the flower too. As the flowers fade they turn more creamy yellow in colour, in fact some varieties are yellow. If this is the case then you can mix together some sunflower and edelweiss to colour all the petals to the depth required. Allow the flower to dry and then steam gently to create a waxy finish.

LEAVES

18 Roll out some well-kneaded mid-green flowerpaste leaving a thick ridge for the wire – a grooved board can be used successfully for this job. Cut out a basic ovate-shaped leaf using the plain-edge cutting wheel.

OUTER PETALS

14 The number of outer petals varies. To make a half-open gardenia I use six petals using either the same sized cutter as previously or more often I use the next size up in the set (or use the gardenia petal templates on page 141). To make a more open flower I make yet another six petals using the largest petal cutter. Use a 30- or a 28-gauge white wire for a larger petal – soften, vein, wire and curl the left-hand edge as created previously.

19 Insert a moistened 28-, 26- or 24-gauge wire depending on the size of the leaf. The wire should support about half the length of the leaf. Place the leaf onto a foam pad or in your palm and soften the edges, working half on the paste and half on your hand, with a metal ball tool.

20 Texture the leaf using the double-sided gardenia leaf veiner. Remove the leaf from the veiner and then, if you wish, hollow out the back of the leaf very slightly (this does vary between varieties). Pinch the leaf from the base through to the tip to accentuate the central vein.

21 Dust in layers with forest, moss, foliage and vine green. The smaller new growth foliage tends to be a much brighter green than the larger leaves. The backs of the leaves are paler than the top. Tape over each leaf stem with half-width nile green tape.

22 Leave to dry and then dip into a three-quarter glaze or spray with edible spray varnish to create fairly glossy foliage.

Golden gardenia

This is an African single form of gardenia that is much quicker and simpler to make than the more common varieties. The flowers occur in white, cream and yellow, working through to orange colouring.

MATERIALS
24-, 26- and 28-gauge wires
Pale green and pale yellow flowerpaste
Seed-head stamens
White and nile green floristry tape
Sunflower, edelweiss, vine, forest, foliage, daffodil and aubergine petal dusts

EQUIPMENT
Curved gardenia petal cutters or Australian rose petal cutters
Rolling pin
Non-stick board
Cupped Christmas rose or stargazer B petal veiner (SKGI) or anemone petal veiner (ALDV)
Gardenia leaf veiner (SKGI)
Dusting brushes
Dresden tool

PISTIL AND STAMEN
1 These are made in the same way as the open gardenia centre (see steps 10 and 11 on page 41). Colour the tips of the stamens with sunflower and a little aubergine petal dust.

PETALS
2 There can be between 5 and 12 petals on this form of gardenia. The size of flower varies quite a bit too. Roll out some pale yellow flowerpaste, leaving a thick ridge for the wire.

3 Insert a short length of 28-gauge white wire into about a third of the ridge. Soften the edges and vein using one of the petal veiners listed above. Repeat to make the required number of petals. Curl the back of the petal with the dresden tool as described for the gardenia (see step 8 on page 41).

4 Tape the petals around the stamens and pistil using half-width white floristry tape. Add a ball of yellow paste and work it into a slender neck on the back of the flower.

COLOURING
5 Dust the petals and the back of the flower to your requirements – here I have used a mixture of edelweiss, a touch of daffodil and quite a bit of sunflower petal dusts. Add tinges of vine green/foliage to the base of the neck. Add a calyx as described for the gardenia (see step 4 on page 40).

BUDS
6 The buds are much longer and very slender. Bend a hook in the end of a 24-gauge wire. Attach a cone of pale yellow paste and thin down the base to create the long neck shape. Pinch several petals from the broader upper section and spiral as described for the gardenia (see steps 1 and 2 on page 40). Dust as for the flower and add the calyx. The leaves are made in the same way as on pages 42–3 (steps 18 to 22).

Trailing succulent

Senecio radicans has a wonderful trailing nature that works well with sprays, bouquets and arrangements. On occasion I have been known to make these when travelling as a passenger on long car journeys as they require very little effort or equipment. There is another Senecio that I am fond of making too – its common name is string of pearls. In my classes the succulents have been nicknamed 'the flirts' as they are addictive to make!

MATERIALS
33- or 35-gauge white wires
Pale green flowerpaste
Nile green floristry tape
Forest, foliage, vine, edelweiss and
   aubergine petal dusts
Edible spray varnish (Fabilo)

EQUIPMENT
Wire cutters
Fine-nose pliers
Plain-edge cutting wheel (PME) or sharp
   scalpel
Large dusting brush

LEAVES

1 Cut several short lengths of 35- or 33-gauge white wire – the finer the better. Roll small balls of flowerpaste, gradually increasing the size, and then form them into slender cone shapes. Insert a moistened wire into the ball and work the base of the cone into a slight point at the base, onto the wire. Curve the tip slightly using fine-nose pliers.

2 Mark a central vein down the curved upperside of the leaf using a plain-edge cutting wheel or a sharp scalpel – this vein is known as the leaf's window! Repeat to make loads of leaves in varying sizes.

ASSEMBLY

3 The leaves may be dusted prior to assembling the long trails but I prefer to tape them and then dust as they are much easier to control that way. Use a 33-gauge 'leader wire' and tape the leaves onto it using quarter-width nile green tape. Start with the smallest leaves. Leave a little of each individual wire on show and make sure that their 'windows' are facing towards the light.

COLOURING

4 Use a mixture of foliage, a touch of forest and edelweiss to dust the leaves. Add touches of vine green and aubergine if desired. Glaze lightly with edible spray varnish.

Smilax

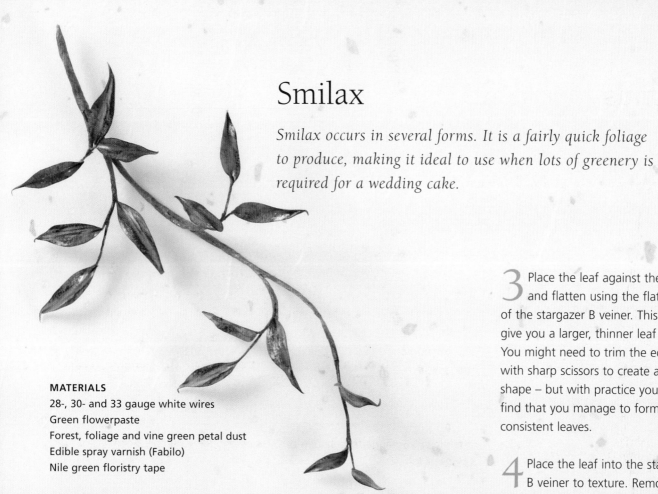

Smilax occurs in several forms. It is a fairly quick foliage to produce, making it ideal to use when lots of greenery is required for a wedding cake.

MATERIALS
28-, 30- and 33 gauge white wires
Green flowerpaste
Forest, foliage and vine green petal dust
Edible spray varnish (Fabilo)
Nile green floristry tape

EQUIPMENT
Wire cutters
Non-stick board
Stargazer B petal veiner (or similar)
Sharp scissors
Flat dusting brushes

CLADODES

1 These look like the leaves of the plant but they are actually modified flattened stems that produce tiny white flowers often followed by red berries. In the remainder of the text they will be referred to as leaves! Cut short lengths of 33-, 30- or 28-gauge white wire – the size of the wire depends upon the size of leaf you plan to make.

2 Roll a ball of green flowerpaste and then form it into a slender carrot shape. Insert a wire into the broad end of the carrot. Work the paste onto the wire and into a smooth shape rolling it between your palms.

3 Place the leaf against the board and flatten using the flat side of the stargazer B veiner. This should give you a larger, thinner leaf shape. You might need to trim the edges with sharp scissors to create a neater shape – but with practice you will find that you manage to form more consistent leaves.

4 Place the leaf into the stargazer B veiner to texture. Remove from the veiner and pinch the leaf at the base and at the tip to accentuate a central vein.

COLOURING AND ASSEMBLY

5 Dust the leaf lightly with forest green and overdust heavily with foliage and vine green. Spray with edible spray varnish – these leaves should be quite glossy so you might need to apply a couple of light coats to create the desired effect.

6 Tape into sets of three using half-width nile green floristry tape and then continue to tape the leaves onto a longer, stronger wire.

Cotinus

Cotinus provides the flower maker with a very simple yet extremely effective foliage as the leaves of the plant can be a bright fresh green, often tinged with red and also brown and purple, which is great for adding depth to a bouquet or arrangement.

MATERIALS
Pale green flowerpaste
22-, 26-, 28- and 30- gauge wires
Aubergine, African violet, nutkin brown
   and foliage petal dusts
Nile green floristry tape
Edible spray varnish (Fabilo)

EQUIPMENT
Rolling pin
Non-stick board
Rose petal cutters (TT 276-280) or
   bougainvillea cutters (J)
Medium ball tool
Rose leaf or poinsettia leaf veiners (SKGI)

LEAVES

1 Roll out some pale green flowerpaste leaving a thick ridge for the wire. Cut out a leaf shape using one of the rose petal or bougainvillea cutters.

2 Insert a moistened wire – the gauge will depend upon the size of the leaf, 26-gauge for a larger leaf, 28-gauge for a medium and 30-gauge for a small leaf.

3 Soften the edge of the leaf using a medium-sized ball tool. Place in a poinsettia or rose leaf veiner to texture. Pinch the leaf from the base to the tip to accentuate the central vein. Repeat to make the required number of varying-sized leaves.

COLOURING

4 To create depth of colour in the leaves it is best to dust them while the paste is still pliable. Dust with layers of aubergine, African violet and nutkin brown petal dust. It is important to leave the backs of the leaves mostly green although a little of the colour catching the veins can be very effective.

5 Tape over each stem with quarter-width nile green tape and then tape the leaves into fairly tight snug groups using half-width tape. Add these small groups onto a 22-gauge wire to form longer stems if required. Dust the stems with the same colours as the foliage. The leaves are not very shiny so it should be enough to simply steam them (see page 12) or spray very lightly with edible spray varnish.

Ginger lily

This ginger lily (Hedychium gardneranum) is native to the Himalayas. The flowers are smaller with longer stamens than the more common white ginger lily. These wonderfully scented flowers are often available as cut flowers. Although the stems are usually massed with flowers I find them easier to incorporate into sprays and arrangements with fewer flowers. There are white, cream, yellow, orange, pink and coral varieties too.

MATERIALS

20-, 22-, 26-, 28-, 30- and 33-gauge white wires
Pale creamy yellow and green flowerpaste
Sunflower, daffodil, ruby, coral, foliage, aubergine and vine green petal dusts
Isopropyl alcohol
White and nile green floristry tape

EQUIPMENT

Wire cutters
Dusting brushes
Rolling pin
Non-stick board
Simple leaf cutter (TT229, 230) or see the templates on page 141
Stargazer B petal veiner (SKGI)
Curved scissors
Small celstick or smooth ceramic tool
Silk veining tool (HP)
Plain-edge cutting wheel (PME)

PISTIL

1 The pistil is actually a combination of pistil (stigma and style) combined with a fertile stamen (anther and filament). Use a third of a length of a 33-gauge white wire. Attach a ball of pale yellow paste about 4–5 cm (1½–2 in) from the end of the wire and firmly and quickly work the paste to the tip to create a fine smooth coating. Curve the length of the paste into a graceful curve.

2 Form a fine sausage of paste and make sure it is slightly pointed at both ends. Attach to the tip of the coated wire. Allow to dry before colouring. (I often find very fine things like this are easier and stronger if made with cold porcelain, which would allow you to use non-toxic hi-tack glue to hold the paste onto the end of the wire.) Dust the length of the pistil with coral and ruby petal dust. Dilute a little ruby dust with isopropyl alcohol and paint the sausage tip.

PETALS

3 To make life more confusing, what look like the three large petals to this flower are in fact stamenoids – petal-like infertile stamens! To make the instructions simpler to follow I will refer to them as petals. To make the two smaller petals, roll out some pale yellow flowerpaste leaving a thick ridge for the wire. Cut out a petal shape using one of the two sizes of simple leaf cutters – this will depend upon how big you want to make the flower. Insert a moistened 30- or 28-gauge white wire into the ridge from the pointed end of the petal. Work the base of the petal to elongate it slightly.

4 Soften the edges with a ball tool and then texture using the stargazer B petal veiner. Pinch the petal to accentuate the central vein. Curve the petal back slightly. Repeat to make two petals.

5 To make the larger heart-shaped petal roll out some yellow paste to leave a thick ridge. Cut out the petal shape using the simple leaf cutter and insert a 28-gauge wire about half way into the petal. Twist the base to elongate the shape and secure the petal firmly to the wire.

6 Cut the top of the petal into a heart shape using curved scissors. Place the paste back onto the board and broaden each half of the petal using a celstick or smooth ceramic tool.

7 Vein the petal using the stargazer B petal veiner and then place the petal onto your index finger and work the top edges using the silk veining tool to texture and frill the edge slightly. Pinch the central vein and curve the petal back slightly.

NARROW PETALS

8 There are three fine appendages to the flower – these look like bracts but are actually the true petals. These are made using 33-gauge wire. Roll a tiny ball of paste onto the wire and work into a fine elongated petal. Flatten the shape to thin it and then texture with the stargazer B veiner. Pinch from the base to the tip. Repeat to make three – although often these drop off the real flower and one, two or none of them will be present!

COLOURING AND ASSEMBLY

9 Dust all the petals from the base to the tip with a mixture of sunflower and daffodil petal dusts. Add colour from the edges towards the base. Add a tinge of coral at the base of each petal.

10 Tape the heart-shaped petal onto the pistil using quarter-width white floristry tape. Add the two side petals next, followed by the three narrow petals at the base.

11 Blend a ball of yellow paste behind the flower to create the neck. Dust to match the petals.

BUDS

12 Use 28- and 26-gauge white wires for the various sizes of buds. Form a cone shape of yellow paste and insert the wire into the base. Work the paste down the wire to create an elongated bud shape.

13 Pinch three flanges from the tip of the bud to represent the three outer petals. Twist the petals around the tip of the bud to create a spiral look. Dust with daffodil and sunflower petal dusts.

BRACT

14 There is a bract at the base of each bud and flower that conceals the ovary of the flower. I usually only create the bract shape. Roll out some green flowerpaste and cut out a pointed arrowhead shape using the plain-edge cutting wheel. Texture the surface of the bract using the stargazer B veiner and then wrap it around the base of the flower or bud.

15 Dust with vine green and a touch of foliage. Add ruby or aubergine to the edges.

16 Tape the buds to the end of a 20- or 22-gauge wire using half-width nile green tape. Spiral the buds around the stem, gradually introducing the flowers.

Sandersonia

This plant is native to South Africa but it is grown commercially in many countries for the cut-flower market. The plant is related to the more familiar gloriosa lily and is equally as poisonous, so care must be taken when handling fresh specimen flowers. The flowers can be yellow or orange in colour.

MATERIALS
White seed-head stamens
Non-toxic hi-tack craft glue (Impex)
22-, 24-, 26- and 28-gauge white wires
Daffodil, sunflower, coral, vine and
    foliage petal dusts
Creamy yellow and mid-green
    flowerpaste
Fresh egg white
Edible spray varnish (Fabilo)
Nile green floristry tape

EQUIPMENT
Scissors
Wire cutters
Flat dusting brush
Rolling pin
Non-stick board
Sandersonia flower cutter (AD) or see the
    template on page 141 and sharp
    scalpel or plain-edge cutting wheel
Medium metal ball tool
Dresden tool (JEM) or porcupine quill
Celstick
Sandersonia leaf cutters (AD) or see the
    templates on page 141 and sharp
    scalpel or plain-edge cutting wheel
Lily leaf veiner

STAMENS

1 Take three stamens and fold them in half. Bond the fold in the stamens with a small amount of non-toxic hi-tack craft glue. Squeeze the glue into the stamens to flatten them slightly and secure together. Allow to set and trim off the excess from the glued sections.

2 Cut a half length of 24-gauge wire. Apply a little more glue onto the base of the stamens and attach onto the end of the wire. Firmly squeeze the stamens and wire together to secure firmly. Allow to dry. Dust the stamens with vine green and the tips with sunflower petal dust.

3 Add a small ball of green flowerpaste at the base of the stamens to represent the ovary. Allow to dry.

FLOWER

4 Roll out some creamy yellow flowerpaste – not too thinly. Cut out the flower shape using the sandersonia flower cutter or use the template and cut out using a scalpel or plain-edge cutting wheel.

5 Soften the edges of the petals using a medium ball tool. Hollow each section of the shape using a rolling action with the ball tool.

6 Turn the shape over and draw a line to separate each petal using the fine end of the dresden tool or a porcupine quill.

7 Carefully pinch each section at the base to make sharp points and create a gathered effect.

8 Moisten one side of the shape and wrap the two edges together. Place the shape onto a celstick and blend the join by pressing the paste against the celstick with your thumb.

9 Apply a little more egg white to the gathered points of the shape and carefully squeeze the six sections together to form the bell shape of the flower.

10 Pull the stamens through the centre of the flower and pinch the flower firmly against the wire. Allow to dry before dusting with daffodil and sunflower petal dusts mixed together. Tinge with vine green and foliage. A light dusting of coral may also be used to create a warmer colouring.

LEAVES

11 Roll out some mid-green flowerpaste leaving a thick ridge. Cut out the leaf using one of the sandersonia leaf cutters or use the template and cut out using a scalpel or plain-edge cutting wheel.

12 Insert a 26- or 28-gauge wire into the thick ridge – the gauge will depend upon the size of the leaf.

13 Soften the edges with a ball tool. Vein using a lily leaf veiner or create freehand veins using the small wheel of the plain-edge cutting wheel.

14 Pinch the leaf from the base to the tip to accentuate the central vein. Curve into shape.

15 Dust in layers with foliage and vine green. Glaze lightly with edible spray varnish.

ASSEMBLY

16 Tape a few leaves tightly to the end of a 22-gauge wire using half-width nile green floristry tape. Continue to work down the stem, adding buds and gradually flowers.

Full-blown rose

Using this style of rose on a cake adds an instant informal edge to any design. Open roses are much easier to make than standard, styled roses and having each petal individually wired gives more movement too.

MATERIALS

26-, 28- and 30-gauge white wires
White, pale green, holly/ivy and pink
    flowerpaste
Small seed-head stamens
Hi-tack non-toxic craft glue (Impex)
Vine green, white, daffodil, sunflower,
    plum, ruby, nutkin brown, aubergine,
    foliage and forest petal dusts
Nile green floristry tape
Edible spray varnish (Fabilo)

EQUIPMENT

Wire cutters
Fine-nose pliers
Sharp scissors
Tweezers
Dusting brushes
Rolling pin
Non-stick board
Heart-shaped rose petal cutter set (AD)
    or see templates on page 141
Sharp scalpel (optional)
Christmas rose petal veiner (SKGI)
Ball tool
Kitchen paper
Foam pad
Sharp curved scissors
Grooved board
Rose leaf cutters (J)
Large briar rose leaf veiner (SKGI)

STAMENS

1 Cut a half-length of 26-gauge white wire. Bend a small open loop in one end using fine-nose pliers. Bend the loop back against the main length of wire. Hold the hook at the centre with pliers and bend it to form a 'ski' stick. Attach a small amount of pale green paste onto the hook. (I tend to use cold porcelain for this stage, but it's up to you.)

2 Cut some short lengths of seed-head stamens and quickly insert into the soft paste. Allow to dry.

3 You will need a third to half a bunch of stamens to complete the centre for the flower – this will depend upon the size of the flower you are making. Divide the stamens into smaller groups. Line up their tips so that they are evenly positioned. Bond each group together at the centre using hi-tack non-toxic craft glue. Squeeze the glue into the strands of the stamens and flatten them as you work. Leave a short length of stamen at either end unglued. Allow to dry for a few minutes.

4 Cut the stamens in half and trim away the excess to leave short lengths. Attach these small groups around the dried centre using a very small amount of hi-tack non-toxic craft glue. Leave to dry. Curl the stamens using tweezers to create a more relaxed, natural-looking set of stamens.

5 Dust the stamen centre and the length of the stamens with vine green petal dust. Mix together sunflower and daffodil petal dusts and colour the tips of the stamens. Add tinges of nutkin brown and aubergine to the tips if desired.

PETALS

6 I use several sizes of cutter to complete one rose. The number is not an exact measure although I use no fewer than 15 petals for this style of rose and usually try to make 5 petals of each size. Roll out some pink flowerpaste paste leaving a thick ridge for the wire. Cut out the petal using one of the heart-shaped rose petal cutters or use the template on page 141.

7 Insert a moistened wire (the gauge will depend upon the size of the petal). Soften the edge of the petal and then vein using a Christmas rose petal veiner.

8 Hollow out the centre of the petal using a ball tool. Curl back the edges of the petal and leave to firm up slightly in a kitchen-paper ring former. Repeat to make the required number of petals.

COLOURING

9 Mix together white, daffodil, sunflower and a touch of vine green petal dusts and dust a patch of colour at the base of each petal on both sides. Next, dust the petals quite heavily with plum petal dust. Rub the dust onto the petals to create an intense colour. Add some aubergine to the edges of each petal. The back of each petal should be slightly paler.

ASSEMBLY

10 Tape a few of the small petals tightly around the stamens using half-width nile green floristry tape. Continue to add the other petals, gradually increasing the petal size as you build up the flower. It helps if the paste is still slightly pliable at this stage so that you can 'snuggle' the petals together to create a more realistic rose.

CALYX

11 Cut five lengths of 30-gauge white wire. Work a ball of pale green flowerpaste onto the wire creating a long tapered carrot shape. Place the shape against the board and flatten using the flat side of one of the double-sided veiners. If the shape looks distorted simply trim into shape with a pair of sharp scissors.

12 Place the flattened shape onto a foam pad or the palm of your hand and soften and hollow out the length using the ball tool. Pinch the sepal from the base to the tip. Cut fine 'hairs' into the edge of the sepal using a pair of sharp curved scissors. Repeat to make five sepals. I tend to leave one sepal without hairs – although remember there are some varieties of rose that have no hairs to their calyces at all.

13 Dust each sepal on the outer surface with a mixture of foliage and forest green. Add tinges of aubergine mixed with plum or ruby petal dust. Use the same brush used for the green mixture and dust lightly on the inner surface of each sepal with white petal dust. Lightly glaze the back of each sepal with edible spray varnish.

14 Tape the five sepals to the base of the rose, positioning a sepal over a join. Add a ball of paste for the ovary and pinch and squeeze it into a neat shape.

LEAVES

15 Roll out some holly/ivy flowerpaste, leaving a thick ridge for the wire (a grooved board can speed up this process greatly). Cut out the leaves using the rose leaf cutters. (You will find that the black rose leaf set does not allow for very thick leaves – these tend to stick in the cutter.) Insert a moistened 26-, 28- or 30-gauge wire into the leaf depending on its size.

16 Soften the edge of the leaf and vein using the large briar rose leaf veiner. Pinch from behind the leaf to accentuate the central vein and give more movement to the leaf. Repeat to make leaves of various sizes. Tape over a little of each wire stem with quarter-width nile green tape. Tape the leaves into sets of three or five, starting with the largest leaf and two medium-sized leaves, one on either side. Finally add the two smaller leaves at the base.

17 Dust the edges with aubergine and plum or ruby dusts mixed together. Use this colour on the upper stems too. Dust the upper surface of the leaf in light layers with forest green and more heavily with foliage and vine green. Dust the backs with white petal dust using the brush used for the green colours. Spray with edible spray varnish.

Egyptian fan orchid

This is based on an orchid called bulbophyllum. I have added a twist of artistic licence to make this flower a bit more user friendly. I like the fan shapes that these collective orchids make and so have nicknamed it the Egyptian fan orchid. They are very useful for adding a touch of drama to a spray or arrangement.

MATERIALS

White flowerpaste

22- and 33-gauge wire

White and nile green floristry tape

Plum, African violet and aubergine petal dusts

Isopropyl alcohol, to dilute plum petal dust

EQUIPMENT

Rolling pin

Non-stick board

Single daisy petal cutter

Sharp scalpel (optional)

Stargazer B petal veiner (SKGI)

Plain-edge cutting wheel

Fine-nose pliers

Sharp fine scissors

Dusting brushes

Stencil brush/new toothbrush

LATERAL SEPALS

1 These are fused together into one large, almost split, daisy-like petal. Roll out some white paste leaving a thick ridge at the centre. Cut out the petal shape using a large daisy petal cutter. Cut into the thick ridge using a sharp scalpel or fine scissors.

2 Insert a 33-gauge wire into each of the two split thick areas. This can be a bit tricky to deal with at first. Soften the edges and then vein using the stargazer B petal veiner. Add extra veins using the plain-edge cutting wheel. Twist the wired sections back onto themselves and tape the two wires together using quarter-width white floristry tape. Use fine scissors to make a small V-shaped cut at the tip of the petal. Leave to dry.

3 Dust with a mixture of plum and African violet petal dusts. Add tinges of aubergine at the base.

COLUMN, LABELLUM AND LATERAL PETALS

4 Attach a tiny cone of paste to the end of a 33-gauge wire. Hollow out the underside and leave to dry.

5 Make the labellum and lateral petals from tiny teardrop-shaped pieces of paste. Flatten them and pinch onto the column.

DORSAL

6 Make in the same way as the labellum and lateral petals, but it is much larger and curves over the rest of the smaller petals.

7 Dust the whole of this section with aubergine. Tape onto the base of the daisy-shaped petal.

8 Repeat to make several orchids and tape them in a fan formation onto a 22-gauge wire using half-width nile green floristry tape.

9 Add tiny spots of colour by loading a stencil brush/new toothbrush with diluted plum petal dust. Flick colour all over the orchids.

Eyelash orchid

*This orchid is made using freehand techniques. It is based on
one of the South American Epidendrum orchids, with a touch
of artistic licence added to speed up the flower-making process!*

MATERIALS
26-, 28- and 33-gauge
   white wires
White and pale green
   flowerpaste
Fresh egg white
Nile green floristry tape
White, vine green, plum, foliage
   and aubergine petal dusts
Edible spray varnish (Fabilo)

EQUIPMENT
Wire cutters
Non-stick board
Stargazer B petal veiner (SKGI)
Sharp scissors
Dresden tool (JEM)
Fine curved scissors
Plain-edge cutting wheel (PME)
Sharp scalpel

OUTER PETALS
1 Cut some 33-gauge wire into
thirds. Roll a small ball of well-
kneaded white flowerpaste and insert
a dry wire into it. Work the paste
down the wire firmly between your
finger and thumb to create a fine
elongated carrot shape. The size of
the orchid varies so it does not matter
too much about the exact length just
as long as you are fairly consistent
with all five petals.

2 Smooth the length of the petal
between your palms and then
place against a non-stick board.
Flatten the petal using the flat side
of the petal veiner.

3 Pick up the flattened petal shape
from the board and if the edges
are uneven simply trim them with a
sharp pair of scissors. Place the petal
into the stargazer B veiner and
squeeze both sides of the veiner
to firmly texture the petal.

4 Pinch the petal from the base to
the tip to emphasize the central
vein. Curve the petal. Repeat to make
five.

LABELLUM
5 Repeat the above process to
create the lip. Use slightly more
paste to create a longer petal shape.
Try to leave a broader section at the
base of the petal. Flatten and vein
using the stargazer B veiner.

6 Place the lip onto the board and work the broad section at the base of the petal using the broad end of the dresden tool. This thins out the section to create a frilly effect. Cut into the section with a fine pair of curved scissors to create the fringed 'eyelash' effect required. Pinch and curve the length of the lip.

ASSEMBLY

8 Tape two of the outer petals onto either side of the lip petal using quarter-width tape. Add the three remaining petals behind these two to complete the shape. If the paste is still pliable at this stage it will enable you to reshape and position the petals to create a more relaxed flower.

LEAVES

11 Roll out some green flowerpaste leaving a thick ridge for the wire. Cut out a freehand leaf shape. Insert a 28- or 26-gauge wire depending upon the size of the leaf. Soften the edge and then texture using the stargazer B petal veiner.

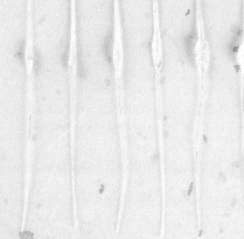

COLUMN

7 Roll a small sausage of white flowerpaste and attach at the base of the lip using a tiny amount of fresh egg white. Quickly open up the broader tip of the column using the broad end of the dresden tool. As you do this support the back of the column between your finger and thumb – this also helps to create a 'backbone' ridge to the shape.

9 Dust the outer petals with a light mixture of vine green and white petal dust. Tinge the edges with aubergine and plum mixed together.

10 There is a long back to this orchid which is optional. Simply add a sausage of white flowerpaste onto the back and work it around the wire to neaten the join in the back of the petals. Draw a few fine lines down the length of the back using the plain edge-cutting wheel. Dust as for the outer petals.

12 Pinch the leaf to accentuate a central vein. Curve and allow to firm up a little before dusting.

13 Dust with layers of foliage and vine green petal dusts. Add an aubergine tinge to the edge of the leaf. Spray lightly with edible spray varnish.

Spider orchid

This is a pretty, small, quick orchid with more than a dash of artistic licence added! I find these a very useful addition to a spray or arrangement – they add interesting texture and allow the use of fairly strong colours.

FLOWERS

MATERIALS
Pale yellow flowerpaste
35-, 33-, 30- and 26-gauge white wires
Fresh egg white
Sunflower, tangerine, coral, ruby, aubergine, vine and foliage petal dusts
Poinsettia red and cyclamen liquid food colours
Nile green floristry tape

EQUIPMENT
Wire cutters
Cupped Christmas rose petal veiner (SKGI)
Dresden tool (Jem)
Dusting brushes
Fine paintbrush
Plain-edge cutting wheel

COLUMN AND LIP/LABELLUM

1 To make the column simply attach a tiny ball of paste to the end of a short length of 35- or 33-gauge white wire. Work the paste down the wire to form a slender cone shape. Hollow out one side and curve slightly. Leave to dry.

2 To create the lip form another cone shape and then thin down the broad end slightly too. Flatten and thin the shape using the flat side of the Christmas rose petal veiner.

3 Frill the edge of the petal using the broad end of the dresden tool. Attach the petal to the base of the column using a tiny amount of fresh egg white. Leave to dry before dusting in layers with sunflower, tangerine, coral and ruby. Add tiny spots to the lip with a mixture of poinsettia and cyclamen liquid food colours using a fine paintbrush.

OUTER PETALS AND SEPALS

4 The two wing petals and three outer sepals are all made in the same way. Use 35- or 33-gauge wire and blend a tiny amount of yellow paste on the end to create the length of petal required – this type of orchid can vary so the length is up to you. Smooth the paste and then flatten and vein using the cupped Christmas rose petal veiner. Pinch the petal/sepal to create a central vein.

5 Dust as for the lip and tape around the dried lip. Create a series of fine tapered buds mounted on 33- and 30-gauge wires. Divide the surface into three using the plain-edge cutting wheel. Curve slightly and dust to match the flowers.

6 Starting with a tiny bud, tape it onto the end of a 26-gauge wire using quarter-width nile green tape. Increase the bud size working down the stem and then introduce the flowers. Dust the stem with vine green, foliage and a little aubergine.

Dischidia

Native to South East Asia and Australia, the genus Dischidia comprises about 80 species. The foliage can be very decorative or fairly simple in form as shown here. The trailing nature of the plant makes it ideal for use in sprays and bouquets.

MATERIALS
30-, 33- and 35-gauge white wires
Pale green flowerpaste
Nile green floristry tape
Forest, foliage, edelweiss and aubergine
  petal dusts
Edible spray varnish (Fabilo)

EQUIPMENT
Wire cutters
Non-stick board
Leaf veiner (optional)
Dusting brushes
Fine-nose pliers

LEAVES

1 Cut several short lengths of fine wire. The gauge of wire you use will depend upon the size of foliage you are making. Roll a small ball of well-kneaded pale green flowerpaste and then form it into a cone shape.

2 Insert a moistened wire into the base. Work the base into a slight point. Pinch the sides of the cone slightly and then place against the non-stick board and flatten with your fingers or use the smooth side of a veiner.

3 Pinch the leaf at the base and the tip. Repeat to make a number of leaves, starting with tiny ones and then gradually increase them to the required size.

ASSEMBLY AND COLOURING

4 Tape the leaves to a 33-gauge wire using quarter-width nile green floristry tape. Use one leaf or use them in pairs. Start with very small leaves and gradually increase the size down the stem. These trails of foliage can be very long. Fine-nose pliers can help to create a tight, neat finish.

5 Dust lightly with a mixture of edelweiss, foliage and forest green. Add tinges of aubergine if desired. Spray the leaves very lightly with edible spray varnish.

Cosmos

There are about 26 species in the Cosmos family. The family originates from Mexico although the plants have naturalized themselves in many other parts of the world. Commonly the flowers are white, pink or lavender but there are also red, orange, yellow and dark chocolate-coloured varieties. For the brave at heart there are also semi-double and double forms!

MATERIALS
White seed-head stamens
Non-toxic hi-tack craft glue (Impex)
White or pale pink, and pale green
   flowerpaste
22-, 26-, 28-, 30-, 33- and 35-gauge white
   wires
Plum, aubergine, African violet, foliage
   and vine green petal dusts
Nile green floristry tape

EQUIPMENT
Fine sharp scissors
Australian rose petal set (TT349-352) or
   see Australian rose templates
   on page 140
Rolling pin
Non-stick board
Dresden tool (J)
Ball tool
Small cosmos petal veiner (SKGI)
Dusting brushes
Plain-edge cutting wheel
Wire cutters

CENTRE

1 The centre can be made with solid flowerpaste but I prefer to use seed-head stamens to give a more freestyle feel to the flower. You will need to use about a quarter to half bunch of seed-head stamens to create the centre. Divide the stamens into smaller groups and line up the tips so that they are roughly the same height in each group. Bond each group at the centre using non-toxic hi-tack glue. Squeeze the glue into the length of the stamens to create an even line but make sure the tips and a little of the length is left unglued to create a natural finish in the final centre. Allow the glue to set a little and then cut the stamens in half and trim off the excess to create fairly short stamens that are held together by a fine line of glue.

PETALS

2 You may need to adjust the shape of the rose petal cutter by squashing it to make a narrow petal (see templates on page 140). Roll out some white or pale pink flowerpaste, leaving a thick ridge for the wire.

3 Cut out the petal shape using the largest of the Australian rose petal cutters. Moisten a 28-gauge white wire and insert into about a third to half the length of the thick ridge in the petal. Pinch the base to secure it to the wire.

COLOURING

6 For a white flower dust a patch of plum petal dust on both sides at the base of each petal. For a pink flower use plum dust and perhaps add a tinge of aubergine or African violet at the base. The back is much paler than the front.

CALYX

8 There are two layers of calyces. I prefer to make each sepal individually but you can also use an eight-petal daisy cutter if you prefer. Form eight small, fine, teardrop shapes of green paste and then flatten each of them. Mark a single line down the length of each and attach this side against each petal.

4 Place the petal topside down and work the top edge into three or four rough points using the broad end of the dresden tool. Soften the side edges of the petal using a ball tool.

5 Vein the petal using the double-sided cosmos petal veiner. Remove from the veiner and curl the edges backwards or forwards slightly, depending on the look you want – gradually unfurling or open and sunning itself! Make eight petals.

ASSEMBLY

7 Tape the eight petals around the stamens using quarter-width nile green floristry tape. Keep the petals quite high up against the stamens, adding a 22-gauge wire to elongate the stem. If the petals are still soft at this stage you will be able to add movement to the flower or decide if you want to close the petals in tighter to represent a just-opening flower. Leave to dry and then steam to set the colour.

9 The second layer can be made with paste but these are finer and longer than the first calyx so you might prefer to use eight twisted lengths of quarter-width nile green floristry tape instead. Whichever you decide on, position these sepals in between those of the first layer. Dust with vine green and foliage. Tinges of aubergine can work wonders too.

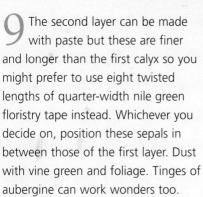

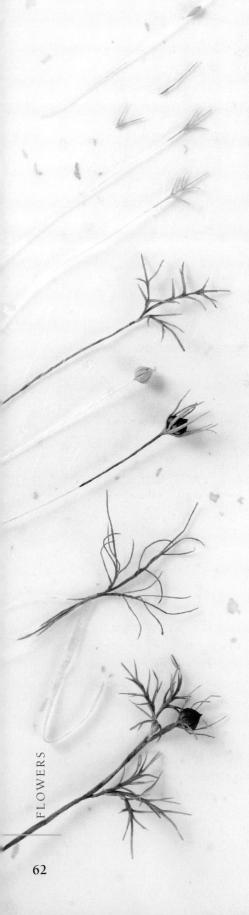

BUDS

10 Roll a ball of green paste and insert a hooked, moistened 26-gauge wire into the base. Pinch the ball to secure it to the wire. Use a plain-edge cutting wheel or sharp scalpel to divide the surface into eight sections. Indent each section using the broad end of the dresden tool. This represents the first layer of sepals. Dust with foliage, vine and aubergine petal dusts. Add an outer calyx as for the flower.

LEAVES

11 These leaves can be made with floristry tape or rolled sections of flowerpaste – the latter is very fragile but very effective. If you decide you are brave enough to tackle the paste version then you will need short lengths of 35- or 33-gauge wire. Work a tiny amount of green paste onto the end of a wire, forming a fine strand with a fine end. Roll a separate fine strand of paste and fold in half and then attach at the base of the central wired strand.

12 Flatten the sections slightly and, if you feel confident, cut into each section with a fine pair of scissors to create a more frond-like finish. Repeat this process to make several leaf sections and then tape together using quarter-width nile green floristry tape.

13 Dust very carefully with foliage, vine and tinges of aubergine petal dusts. The tape version is constructed in a similar way but using twisted strands of quarter-width floristry tape instead.

14 Tape the buds and flowers together, adding sets of foliage in various sizes every time you join a bud or flower onto the main stem. Add a stronger wire for support if needed. Dust the main stem with foliage and vine green. Add a little aubergine to one side of the stem – this is usually where the sunlight hits the plant.

Zinnia

Originally from Mexico, the zinnia is grown worldwide. Their bright and brash colour combinations are wonderful to reproduce in sugar and cold porcelain. There are many varieties of zinnias, with some forming double flowers. I have kept my version as a simple single variety. The centre of the zinnia is very time consuming to make as it is made up of tiny individual flowers.

MATERIALS

Yellow and green cold porcelain
22-, 26-, 28- and 30-gauge white wires
Green sisal
Non-toxic hi-tack glue (Impex)
Sunflower, vine, foliage, coral, tangerine, plum, ruby and aubergine petal dusts
White and green flowerpaste
Nile green floristry tape
Fresh egg white

EQUIPMENT

Celstick or ceramic silk veining tool
Fine sharp scissors
Fine-nose pliers
Dusting brushes
Rolling pin
Non-stick board
Single petal daisy cutter
Plain-edge cutting wheel (PME)
Small ball tool
Wire cutters
8-petal daisy cutter
Heart-shaped rose petal cutter (AD) or see templates on page 141
Mock orange leaf veiner (SKGI)

CENTRE

1 Although the centre can be made with flowerpaste I prefer to make it with cold porcelain as the individual flowers are very fiddly to make and are also quite fragile. Roll a tiny ball of yellow cold porcelain and then form it into a cone shape.

2 Open up the broad end of the cone using the pointed end of a celstick or ceramic tool. Using fine sharp scissors, cut the edge to create five petals.

3 Pinch each petal between your finger and thumb to create five pointed petal shapes. Flatten each petal in turn between your finger and thumb. Repeat to make numerous flowers and leave to dry.

4 Bend a hook in the end of a 22-gauge wire using fine-nose pliers. Attach a ball of green cold porcelain paste onto it. Shred some green sisal (available from art shops and florists). Lightly apply non-toxic hi-tack glue over the ball and roll it in the sisal to texture it. Leave to dry. Dust with vine green and foliage petal dusts.

5 Attach the dried tiny flowers onto the sisal-coated centre using a tiny amount of non-toxic hi-tack glue to hold them in place. Dust the flowers with sunflower petal dust.

OUTER PETALS

6 The number of petals varies between varieties – usually from eight upwards. Roll out some white paste leaving a thick ridge for the wire. Cut out a petal shape using the single petal daisy cutter.

7 Insert a 30- or 28-gauge white wire into the base of the thick ridge on the petal. Hold the petal firmly between your finger and thumb so that the wire does not pierce through the petal.

8 Using a fine pair of scissors, cut a slight indent from the tip of the petal. Use the plain-edge cutting wheel to draw a few veins onto the petal. Turn the petal over and hollow out the underside slightly using a small ball tool. Pinch the petal from the base to the tip to accentuate the central vein. Repeat to make the required number of petals.

COLOURING AND ASSEMBLY

9 Dust the upper surface of the petal with the desired colour of petal dust. Here I have used a mixture of plum, tangerine and coral petal dust. Try to keep the undersides much paler.

10 Tape the petals around the centre using half-width nile green floristry tape. Trim off excess wires as you work to cut down on some of the bulk behind the flower.

CALYX

11 Roll a ball of green flowerpaste and form it into a long teardrop shape. Pinch out the broad end so that the shape looks like a wizard's hat. Thin out the brim using a celstick or ceramic tool. Cut out the calyx shape using the 8-petal daisy cutter. Soften each petal and then draw a line down each to create central veins. Open up the centre of the calyx using the pointed end of a celstick.

12 Roll out some more green paste and cut out another calyx shape using the 8-petal daisy cutter. Soften and vein as before and then place on top of the first calyx, making sure that the sepals are positioned to cover a join in the first layer.

13 Carefully thread the calyx onto the back of the flower using a little fresh egg white to secure it in place. Work the neck of the calyx to refine it slightly. Trim off the excess.

14 Dust with foliage and vine green petal dusts. Add tinges of aubergine to the edges.

FOLIAGE

15 Roll out some green paste leaving a ridge for the wire. Cut out the leaf shape using the heart-shaped rose petal cutter or the heart-shaped rose petal templates on page 141. Insert a moistened 28- or 26-gauge white wire into the thick ridge. Soften the edges and then vein using the mock orange leaf veiner. Repeat to make leaves in pairs.

16 Dust with foliage and vine green. Add a tinge of ruby/aubergine to the edges. Tape in pairs down the flower stems. Dust the stem as for the leaves.

Anemone

Native to Mediterranean countries and also parts of Asia, the anemone has been cultivated since ancient times. They are wonderful to make in sugar because of their intense colouring and beautiful stamen-packed centres.

MATERIALS

22-, 26- and 28-gauge white wires
Pale green cold porcelain (optional)
Semolina coloured with black and deep
  purple petal dusts
White seed-head stamens
Hi-tack non-toxic craft glue (Impex)
African violet, plum, aubergine, ruby,
  black, foliage, forest and vine green
  petal dusts
Clear alcohol (Cointreau or kirsch)
White and pale green flowerpaste
Pale green or white floristry tape
Edible spray varnish (Fabilo)
Fresh egg white

EQUIPMENT

Fine-nose pliers
Sharp fine curved scissors
Sharp scissors
Tweezers
Rolling pin
Non-stick board
Grooved board
Anemone petal and leaf cutter set (AD)
  or see templates on page 140
Sharp scalpel
Foam pad
Large ball tool
Anemone petal veiner (Aldaval)
Kitchen paper
Wild geranium leaf veiner (SKGI)
  dresden tool

CENTRE AND STAMENS

1 The centre of the flower can be made with flowerpaste however, I prefer to use craft glue to bond the stamens around the centre to create a neater finish so it is advisable to make an inedible centre using cold porcelain instead. Bend a hook in the end of a 22-gauge wire using fine-nose pliers. Roll a ball of pale green cold porcelain and insert the hooked wire into it. Pinch the ball onto the wire to secure in place. Texture the surface of the ball using the curved scissors. Moisten the surface of the ball and dip into the coloured semolina. Shake off the excess and leave to dry.

2 Make several small groups of seed-head stamens. Line up their tips at both ends. Use a little non-toxic craft glue at the centre of each bunch to bond the stamens together. Work the glue from the centre towards the tips leaving a little of the stamen length unglued at each end to create movement in the finished flower. Flatten the glue into the stamens and leave to set – it will only take about 4–5 minutes for the glue to firm up sufficiently. Cut the stamens in half using sharp scissors and trim off the excess length – the stamens should be a little longer than the black centre.

3 Apply a little glue to each cropped stamen group and attach around the base of the black centre to create a neat ring. Leave to dry, and then pinch with tweezers to create a little movement and realism. Dust the stamens to match

the flower – a purple flower has purple stamens, a red flower has red stamens etc. Dilute a little black petal dust with clear alcohol and add a touch of deep purple petal dust to create a thick paint to colour the tips of the stamens. Leave to dry.

6 Place the petal onto a foam pad and soften the edges with a large ball tool. Texture the petal using a double-sided anemone petal veiner or something with a similar fine fan formation texture. Hollow the centre of the petal very gently and allow to firm up a little in a kitchen-paper ring former. Repeat to make the required number of petals.

ASSEMBLY

8 Start by taping the smaller petals onto the stamens using half-width white or pale green floristry tape. Continue to add the larger petals a few at a time to build up the complete flower head. You will find that some flowers look better with fewer petals and some with more. Tape over the stem a few times to create a fleshy stem.

PETALS

4 Roll out some white paste leaving a ridge thick enough to insert a fine wire. (A grooved board may also be used for this job.) Cut out a petal shape using one of the anemone petal cutters or use a sharp scalpel and one of the templates on page 140. The number of petals can vary on each flower. I usually use between 5 and 15 petals per flower and vary the size a little.

5 Insert a 28-gauge wire into the thick ridge so that it supports a third to half a length of the petal.

COLOURING

7 It is best to dust the petals while the paste is still pliable to create strong colouring. In this example I used African violet and plum petal dust to create a very intense purple flower. It is important to leave a white area at the base and use less on the back of the petal. (If you make a mistake and colour the whole petal it is possible to remove a bit of colour with an anti-bacterial wipe.)

10 Using a sharp scalpel or fine scissors make a series of V-shaped cuts in the edge of the leaf to make a finer effect. The edge may also be worked on using the broad end of the dresden tool to create a 'frillier' effect. Repeat to make three leaves for each flower and bud.

11 Dust the edges of each leaf with a little of the flower colour plus a tinge of aubergine. Next, dust in layers from the base with foliage green, adding a touch of forest green, fading the colour a little towards the edges. Overdust with vine green. Glaze lightly with an edible spray varnish or dip into a quarter glaze. Leave to dry.

12 Tape three or four leaves behind the flower so that they are all at the same level on the stem. The more mature the flower, the further down the stem the leaves will be. Dust the stem lightly with foliage, vine, aubergine and perhaps a little of the flower colour too.

BUD

13 Bend a hook in the end of a 20-gauge wire. Form a ball of white paste into an almost egg shape. Moisten, and insert the hook into the broad base of the bud. Leave to dry. Roll out some white paste and cut out five petals using the smaller anemone petal cutter. Soften the edges of each petal and vein using the anemone petal veiner.

14 Moisten the bud with fresh egg white and position the petals around the centre in a fairly informal way, adding them opposite each other. Flatten the bud shape if a tighter bud is required. Dust to match the flower, remembering that the back of the petals is usually paler than the inside. Add leaves as for the flower.

LEAVES

9 Roll out some pale green paste leaving a thick ridge for the wire. Cut out the leaf shape using an anemone leaf cutter. Insert a moistened 26-gauge wire into the thick ridge so that it supports quite a bit of the length in the central section. Soften the edge of the leaf using a large ball tool. Vein the leaf using a wild geranium leaf veiner.

FLOWERS

Hydrangea

There are many species of hydrangea. Here are the instructions for a crimped-edged variety. The decorative bracts of the hydrangea are formed into three, four or more sections looking rather like flower petals. The real flowers are actually tiny and are at the heart of the flower head.

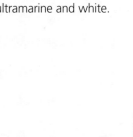

MATERIALS

20-, 22-, 24-, 26-, 28-, 30-, 33- and
   35-gauge white wires
White and green flowerpaste
White and nile green floristry tape
African violet, aubergine, vine green,
   foliage, bluegrass, ultramarine, forest,
   plum and edelweiss white petal dusts
Clear alcohol
Half glaze or edible spray varnish (Fabilo)

EQUIPMENT

Wire cutters
Fine-nose pliers
Sharp scalpel or plain-edge cutting wheel
Dusting brushes
Crimped hydrangea petal cutters (AD) or
   hydrangea petal cutters (TT764, 765)
Medium metal ball tool
Hydrangea petal veiner (SKGI)
New fine toothbrush
Virginia creeper leaf cutters (AD)
Foam pad
Small, medium and large hydrangea leaf
   veiners (SKGI)
Edible spray varnish

BUDS

1 There are a mass of buds and flowers at the heart of the hydrangea and at the centre of each set of decorative bracts. I choose to make only the buds as they are much quicker to make than the tiny flowers. You will need to allow plenty of time to sit and make lots of buds. Cut several short lengths of 35- or 33-gauge white wires. Make a tiny hook in the end of each using fine-nose pliers. Roll several small balls of white paste and insert a dry, hooked wire into each. Work the base of the bud onto the wire to secure it in place.

2 Divide the bud into four or five sections using a sharp scalpel or plain-edge cutting wheel – the number varies on one flower head. Tape these buds into small groups using quarter-width white floristry tape. Dust as required. I have used a mixture of African violet and plum, with tinges of vine green and foliage. For the plain-edged blue hydrangea use a mixture of ultramarine and white.

MODIFIED BRACTS

3 At first glance these look like petals but they are actually modified decorative bracts. They occur in sets of three, four, five or even double forms. I usually use sets of three and four. Roll out some well-kneaded white flowerpaste leaving a thick ridge for a fine wire. Cut out a bract shape using one of the hydrangea petal cutters. Insert a moistened 30- or 28-gauge wire into the thick ridge so that it supports about a third to half the length.

4 Soften the edge of the bract using a medium-sized metal ball tool. Texture the bract in the double-sided hydrangea bract/petal veiner. Pinch the base of the bract to the tip to accentuate a central vein. Repeat to make the required number of bracts. The bracts can be all the same size or you can combine two small and two large.

COLOURING AND ASSEMBLY

5 Tape three or four bracts around a single bud using quarter-width white floristry tape. If you have varied the size then add the two small bracts first opposite each other followed by the two larger ones behind to fill the gaps.

6 Dust the bracts as required. Here I have used patches of various colours – vine green mixed with a little edelweiss and then touches of bluegrass followed by a mixture of plum and African violet. Use ultramarine blue for the blue hydrangea pictured.

7 Tape a small group of buds onto the back of each of the bract flowers. Then start to build up the flower head, taping the flowers onto the end of a 20-gauge wire with nile green floristry tape. Add a group of buds and carry on adding further groups around this central one. Gradually encircle with the bract flowers to complete the flower head.

8 Dilute some African violet petal dust with clear alcohol. Load a new toothbrush with the dark purple colour and flick it over the whole flower head to add dark purple spots.

LEAVES

9 Roll out some green flowerpaste, leaving a thick ridge for the wire. Cut out the leaf using one of the Virginia creeper leaf cutters. Insert a moistened 28-, 26-, 24- or 22-gauge wire – depending upon the size of leaf you are making – into the thick ridge. Soften the edge using a medium ball tool working half on the paste and half on a pad or your hand. Try not to frill the leaf.

10 Vein the leaf using one of the hydrangea leaf veiners. Pinch the leaf from the base to the tip to accentuate the central vein. Repeat to make graduating sizes of foliage.

COLOURING

11 Dust the edges of the leaves with aubergine petal dust. Add a little aubergine towards the base of the leaf also. Dust the upper surface of the leaf in light layers of forest green, from the base fading to the edges, and then heavier with foliage green and finally a little vine green. The backs of the leaves are much paler so use only a little of the colour left on the brush to catch the veins. Allow to dry and then glaze using a half glaze or spray lightly with edible spray varnish.

12 Add the leaves in pairs down the stem, starting with the small leaves and increasing in size as you work down the stem. Dust the main stem with foliage green and a touch of aubergine. Spray the stem with edible spray varnish or steam to seal the colour

Beetleweed

This heart-shaped leaf (Galax urceolata), often used by florists for arrangements and bridal bouquets, is quite leathery in texture. The leaf can be used flat in an arrangement or curled to form interesting spiral effects.

MATERIALS
Mid-green flowerpaste
22-, 24- and 26-gauge white wires
Kitchen paper
Fresh egg white
Foliage, forest, vine green and aubergine
    petal dusts
Edible spray varnish (Fabilo)
Nile green floristry tape

EQUIPMENT
Rolling pin
Non-stick board
Beetleweed leaf cutter set (AD) or see
    templates on page 140
Dresden tool
Very large nasturtium leaf veiner (SKGI)
    or beetleweed leaf veiner (SC)
Large ball tool
Flat dusting brush

CUTTING AND WIRING

1 Roll out some well-kneaded mid-green flowerpaste, leaving a thick ridge for the wire. Cut out the leaf shape using your chosen size of beetleweed cutter or refer to the templates on page 140.

2 Insert a moistened 22-, 24- or 26-gauge wire into the central ridge – the gauge will depend upon the size of the leaf. The leaf needs a fair amount of support especially if it is to curl into a spiral shape.

TEXTURING AND SHAPING

3 Use the broad end of the dresden tool to work the edges of the leaf to break up the regimental serrations to create a more interesting effect.

4 Texture the leaf using the double side nasturtium or beetleweed leaf veiner.

5 If needed, soften the edge using a large ball tool. Pinch the leaf to accentuate the central vein and create 'movement'. Allow to dry supported by some crumpled kitchen paper or roll the leaf up to create a curved, spiral effect. Use little egg white to help hold the shape, along with a sharp pinch at the base to prevent it unravelling. Repeat to make the required number of leaves.

COLOURING AND ASSEMBLY

6 Allow to firm up a little before dusting. Tinge the edges with aubergine petal dust. Use vine green, foliage and a touch of forest green in layers to colour the main body. Dust the back of the leaf lightly using any green colour left on the brush.

7 Allow to dry and then glaze using edible spray varnish. Tape over each stem using half-width nile green floristry tape.

Ornamental grass

I was lucky enough to watch a demonstration by Gregor Lersch – a wonderful florist and flower arranger. He used grasses amongst the flowers and when asked which variety he was using he joked that one was called Grassius Roadside-ius and the other Grassius Carpark-ius! Just after this introduction into the fun side of grasses, three friends of mine created a beautiful wedding cake with roses and grasses.

MATERIALS
25-, 26-, 28-, 30- and 33-gauge white wires
White or pale green flowerpaste
Ruby, aubergine and foliage green
  petal dusts
Edible spray varnish (Fabilo)
Quarter glaze (optional)

EQUIPMENT
Fine curved scissors
Flat dusting brushes

GRASS

1 Choose a wire strong enough to hold the size of grass you intend to make. The one illustrated here was made on 33-gauge wire however, the grasses used in the Metallica bouquet on pages 94–5 were much larger and formed on 28-gauge wires.

2 Blend a small amount of white or pale green flowerpaste onto the end of a wire to create the required length. Hold the wire upside down and quickly snip fine cuts into the paste using a pair of fine curved scissors. Flick some of the cuts back on themselves to open up the shape slightly. Repeat to create a whole bunch of grass. I generally find the more grass used in a bouquet or arrangement the more realistic it looks.

COLOURING

3 Dust as required. Here I have used a touch of foliage green at the base of the grass and then lots of ruby and an overdusting of aubergine. Allow to dry and then spray very lightly with edible spray varnish or dip into a quarter glaze, shake and dry. Use *en masse* for delicate impact.

Rangoon creeper

The Rangoon creeper (Quisqualis indica) is from Tropical Asia – it is also known by the hilarious common name of Drunken Sailor! I came across the plant at the botanical gardens in Christchurch, New Zealand. It is a crazy vine massed with flowers that start off very pale and gradually turn to a peach then coral through to red.

MATERIALS

Fine white stamens

Non-toxic hi-tack craft glue (Impex)

35-, 33-, 30-, 28-, 26-, 24- and 22-gauge white wires

Primrose, coral, red, ruby, white, vine green, foliage and aubergine petal dusts

Pale apricot and pale green flowerpaste

White and nile green floristry tape

Edible spray varnish (Fabilo)

EQUIPMENT

Sharp scissors

Wire cutters

Dusting brushes

Non-stick board

Cupped Christmas rose petal veiner (SKGI)

Medium ball tall

Foam pad

Fine curved scissors

Rolling pin

Plain-edge cutting wheel (PME)

Mandevilla leaf veiner (SKGI)

STAMENS

1 Fold three fine white stamens in half and line up the tips. Remove one tip to leave five stamens. Glue the group together at the bend with hi-tack glue. Leave for a few minutes to dry and then trim off the excess to leave a short group of stamens. Cut a short length of 33-gauge wire and apply a tiny amount of glue to the end. Press the glued wire onto the stamens and pinch them firmly together. Leave to dry and then dust the tips with primrose petal dust.

PETALS

2 Roll a tiny ball of pale apricot flowerpaste and then form it into a cone shape. Insert a short length of 35- or 33-gauge white wire into the base. Work the base of the cone between your finger and thumb to elongate the shape.

3 Place the wired shape onto the non-stick board and flatten it with the smooth side of the Christmas rose petal veiner. At first you might need to trim the shape of the petal slightly but you will gradually start to create more consistent shapes. Soften the edge of the petal using a medium-sized ball tool. Texture the petal using the double-sided Christmas rose veiner.

4 Place the petal on your palm or a foam pad and gently hollow out the back of the petal. Pinch the petal at the base and slightly at the tip to create a little movement. Repeat to make five petals.

COLOURING AND ASSEMBLY

5 The petals can be dusted before or after you assemble the flower – I prefer to tape it together first around the stamens using quarter-width white floristry tape.

6 Dust it as a whole as I find it easier to balance out the colour between petals. Use layers of coral, red and ruby petal dusts to create the depth of colour required. For paler flowers add a touch of white petal dust to the coral. Keep the backs of the petals undusted or very, very pale.

7 Work a ball of very pale green paste at the back of the flower to create a long, slender-necked calyx. Use fine curved scissors to snip a five-sepal calyx, aiming to get a sepal in between a petal. Curve the neck slightly. Dust the calyx very gently with vine green petal dust.

BUDS

8 Cut lengths of 33-, 30- and 28-gauge white wire for the buds (the size of the wire will depend on the size bud you are making). Form a small cone of pale green paste and insert a dry wire into the broad end. Work the base of the bud down onto the wire to create a long, slender neck. Smooth the neck between the fleshy part of your hands. Curve the neck slightly. Snip a quick calyx as for the flower.

9 Dust lightly with vine green. Add a tinge of red to the tip but be careful not to create too much colour – remember the backs of the petals are pale so the bud needs to match.

LEAVES

10 The leaves grow in pairs. Roll out some pale green paste, leaving a thick ridge for the wire. Cut out the leaf using the plain-edge cutting wheel. Insert a 28-, 26- or 24-gauge wire into the thick ridge. Soften the edges and vein using the mandevilla leaf veiner. Pinch the leaf from the base to the tip to accentuate the central vein. Repeat to make the leaves in pairs of graduating sizes.

11 Dust the edges lightly with a mixture of ruby and aubergine. Use layers of foliage and vine green to colour the upper surface of the leaf. Keep the backs a much paler green. Spray lightly with edible spray varnish.

12 Form a trailing stem using a 22-gauge wire. Tape two very small leaves together at the tip of the wire using half-width nile green tape. Leave a gap and then introduce a group of small buds accompanied by a pair of leaves. Continue in this way until you have created the required length.

Brunia seed-heads

There are about seven species of brunia from South Africa.
At first glance the mass of flowers look rather like seed-heads.
The variety pictured here is one of the larger forms.

MATERIALS
24- and 28-gauge wires
Green flowerpaste
Foliage, vine green and aubergine petal
    dusts (white petal and myrtle bridal
    satin, optional)
Edible spray varnish (Fabilo)
Nile green floristry tape

EQUIPMENT
Fine-nose pliers
Fine curved scissors
Dusting brushes

FLOWER HEAD

1 Bend a hook in the end of a 24-gauge white wire using fine-nose pliers. Roll a ball of well-kneaded green flowerpaste. Moisten the hooked wire and insert into the ball, pinching the base of the ball onto the wire to secure it in place.

2 Use a sharp pair of fine curved scissors to snip into the entire surface of the ball to create a rough texture.

3 When the surface is completely textured go back and smooth the cuts slightly by pressing them gently into place. Repeat to make numerous flower heads in varying sizes.

4 Dust to the required depth using foliage, vine and tinges of aubergine. Some brunia varieties have a grey or silver finish to them, which can be created using white petal dust or myrtle bridal satin dust. Spray very lightly with edible spray varnish.

5 Tape the heads into pairs and sets of three using nile green floristry tape.

LEAVES

6 The leaves can be fine or quite heavy and hairy looking. Those used here are a finer form created with lengths of 28-gauge wire taped over with half-width nile green floristry tape. Group several lengths of taped wire together and shape them to create a bit of movement. Snuggle the foliage behind the flower heads. Dust with foliage and vine green. For the larger type of foliage simply coat the wires with green flowerpaste and then snip all over the surface using curved scissors to create a hairy finish.

Geraldton waxplant

This pretty plant from Western Australia produces tiny lilac, rose, red and also white flowers. They are readily available from florists during spring and are useful for bouquets and arrangements.

STAMENS

1 Cut several short lengths of 30- or 28-gauge white wires. Glue a short length of a seed-head stamen onto the end with a touch of hi-tack glue – this represents the pistil. Leave to set and then paint with some diluted aubergine petal dust.

2 Attach five fine stamens around the pistil using a little glue. These should have their tips lower than the tip of the pistil. Dust the tips with plum petal dust and a little touch of vine green at the base.

FLOWER

3 Form a ball of white paste into a cone and then pinch the base to form a small hat shape. Roll out the base to thin the brim and then cut out the flower using a five-petal blossom cutter.

4 Hollow out the centre of the flower and soften the petals using the ceramic tool. Moisten the base of the stamens and pull through the centre. Neaten the back. Dust the edges with plum petal dust and the base with vine green and foliage.

5 Make tiny round buds on 35- or 33-gauge wires. Dust to match the flowers.

LEAVES

6 Cut short lengths of 35- or 33-gauge wire. Attach a ball of green paste to the wire and work the paste to form a thin strand. Flatten the leaf using the flat side of any leaf/petal veiner. If needed, use fine sharp curved scissors to tidy up the shape. Next, pinch a central vein. Repeat to make lots of leaves. Dust with moss and foliage petal dusts.

7 Tape the leaves onto a 28-gauge wire using quarter-width nile green floristry tape. Gradually introduce the buds and flowers to snuggle in amongst the foliage.

MATERIALS

28-, 30-, 33- and 35-gauge white wires
Non-toxic hi-tack craft glue (Impex)
White seed-head stamens
Aubergine, plum, vine, moss and foliage petal dusts
Tiny white stamens
White and green flowerpaste
Nile green floristry tape

EQUIPMENT

Wire cutters
Dusting brushes
Rolling pin
Non-stick board
Small five-petal blossom cutter
Smooth ceramic tool
Leaf/petal veiner
Fine sharp curved scissors

Blue butterfly bush

The pretty blooms of Clerodendrum ugandense *are wonderful as filler flowers on a cake where a blue element is needed. In the past I have made this flower as a single cut-out flower. However, it is much easier to wire each petal resulting in a stronger finished flower.*

MATERIALS

Non-toxic hi-tack craft glue (Impex)
White seed-head stamens
28- and 33-gauge white wires
Ultramarine craft dust
African violet, deep purple and edelweiss
    petal dusts
White flowerpaste
Nile green floristry tape

EQUIPMENT

Scissors
Dusting brushes
Wire cutters
Non-stick board
Stargazer B petal veiner (optional)
Fine-nose pliers
Sharp scalpel
Small metal ball tool

STAMENS

1 Glue together five seed-head stamens with non-toxic hi-tack glue. Make one stamen stand longer than the others to represent the pistil. Cut off the tip of the pistil and when the glue has set cut off the tips from the base too. Glue onto a 33-gauge white wire. Pinch and leave to dry.

2 Curl the stamens. Dust the tips with a mixture of ultramarine craft dust and African violet petal dust. Dust the length of the stamens with the blue mixture mixed with a touch of edelweiss.

PETALS

3 Cut five short lengths of 33-gauge white wire. Attach a ball of well-kneaded white flowerpaste to the end of a wire and work it into a slight point at the tip and taper the base to form a slender neck. Place the shape onto the board and flatten it using the smooth side of the stargazer B petal veiner.

4 Vein the petal using the textured sides of the double-sided veiner and then hollow out the length of the petal using the small metal ball tool. Repeat to make four same-sized petals and one slightly longer petal.

5 Tape the five petals onto the stamens using quarter-width nile green floristry tape, with the longest petal positioned directly opposite the stamens so that they curve towards it.

6 Dust the petals using a mixture of edelweiss, African violet and ultramarine. For the longest petal use a stronger version, omitting the white petal dust.

BUDS

7 Cut short lengths of 28-gauge wires. Bend a hook in the end of each length. Attach a ball of paste to the end of each wire and roll the base slightly to form a neck. Divide the tip into five using a sharp scalpel. Dust with vine green and a little of the blue mixture, plus a touch of deep purple.

Masdevallia orchid

There are many types of masdevallia orchid native to central and South America. The one shown here is a very simple form that is quick, easy and very effective to use on a cake.

LATERAL SEPALS

1 The three petal-like shapes are actually the flower's dorsal and lateral sepals, with the labellum and lateral petals being very tiny at the centre of the flower. They are so tiny that I decided to leave them out and concentrate on the three outer sepals, which makes the process a much quicker one. The three sepals are all made using the same method. You need to make two larger lateral sepals and a much smaller dorsal sepal. Work a ball of well-kneaded white flowerpaste onto a fine wire. Work the paste so that it is broad at the base and very fine at the tip. The wire should support the whole length of the petal.

2 Place the petal against the non-stick board and flatten it using the smooth side of the stargazer B petal veiner – this will thin out the petal and create a much broader shape. With practice the shapes will start to conform to that required, although from time to time you will need to trim the shape with a sharp pair of fine scissors.

3 Soften the edges and then place into the double-sided stargazer B petal veiner to texture. Pinch from the base to the tip to accentuate the central vein. Repeat to make a mirror image pair of lateral sepals. Tape them together with quarter-width white floristry tape.

4 Repeat the process with a 33-gauge wire and less paste to create the dorsal sepal. Tape it tightly onto the lateral sepals and curl the tip.

5 Add a small amount of paste to the back of the flower to create a neck. Blend the paste into the back of the petals using the broad end of the dresden tool. Draw fine lines onto the neck with the plain-edge cutting wheel. Tape over the main stem with quarter-width nile green tape.

COLOURING

6 These orchids can be white, cream, yellow, orange, pink or red, and variations in between, too. I have used layers of plum, African violet and a touch of aubergine to create the flowers shown here.

MATERIALS
White flowerpaste
24-, 30- and 33-gauge white wires
White and nile green floristry tape
Plum, African violet and aubergine petal dusts
Edible spray varnish (Fabilo)

EQUIPMENT
Non-stick board
Stargazer B petal veiner (SKGI)
Sharp fine scissors
Dresden tool
Plain-edge cutting wheel (PME)
Dusting brushes

FLOWERS

Bromeliad foliage

This is the decorative foliage of the flaming sword bromeliad (Vriesea splendens). The plant also produces an eye-catching red flower spike. However, I have one of these plants at home and it has not flowered since I bought it two years ago. I am led to believe that the new growth, which can take about two years to form, will eventually create a new bloom. So while I am still waiting for a bloom to copy here is the foliage, which is actually my favourite part of the plant.

MATERIALS
Pale green flowerpaste
20-, 22- and 24-gauge white wires
Foliage and aubergine petal dusts
Isopropyl alcohol
Edible spray varnish (Fabilo)

EQUIPMENT
Rolling pin
Non-stick board
Plain-edge cutting wheel (PME)
Large tulip leaf veiner (SKGI)
Flat dusting brushes
Fine paintbrush

LEAVES

1 Roll out a large amount of well-kneaded pale green flowerpaste, leaving a long, thick ridge for the wire.

2 Cut out a long, strap-like leaf shape using the large wheel of the plain-edge cutting wheel.

3 Insert a moistened wire into the leaf; the wire gauge will depend upon the size of the leaf you are making. Try to insert the wire into half to three-quarters of the length of the leaf. Place into the tulip leaf veiner and press firmly to impress the fine lines onto the surface of the leaf. (Alternatively you can use a packet of 33-gauge wire to curve and follow the line of the leaf and then press into the surface to vein the back and the front.)

4 Pinch the leaf from the base to the tip to create a bit of movement and curve the tip slightly. Leave to rest for a while to firm up before colouring.

COLOURING

5 Dust the surface of the leaf with foliage petal dust from the edges to the base and from the base to the centre of the leaf using a large flat brush on both the front and the back.

6 Dilute some aubergine petal dust with isopropyl alcohol and paint a series of blotchy stripes at intervals down both sides of the leaf. Once the stripes have dried use a dry brush and aubergine dust to blend and catch the edges of the leaf. This will calm down the painted lines and create a more realistic finish. Leave to dry before spraying with edible spray varnish.

Tillandsia

Another member of the bromeliad Tillandsia, are air plants native to southeast of the USA although most are native to South America. The flowers can be yellow, pink, orange or purple with brightly coloured bracts that look very much like flower petals.

FLOWERS

1 Form three balls of white flowerpaste into cone shapes. Flatten them against the board and roll out each petal in a fan formation using the silk veining tool. Pinch each petal to create a central vein and attach them onto the end of a 28-gauge wire. Twist and blend the base of each petal onto the wire. Curl the tips back slightly.

2 Allow the paste to firm up a little before colouring. Here I used African violet however, you can colour them pink, yellow, orange or purple.

BRACTS

3 Twist a length of half-width white floristry tape and stretch it slightly to create a subtle point. Trim off the extreme twisted section to leave a neat point. Repeat to make numerous bracts. Tape a few onto the back of the flower, gradually working down the stem as you add them.

4 Dust the bracts with plum petal dust. Dust the stem with a little of the bract colour and add tinges of foliage green mixed with white.

LEAVES

5 Use a 35- or 33-gauge white wire for the leaves. Work a tiny ball of pale green flowerpaste onto the wire and work it towards the end of the wire so that most or all of the length is supported. Smooth the paste between your palms and then flatten against the board using the flat side of the stargazer B veiner. Place in the veiner to texture and pinch the leaf from the base to the tip to create a central vein, twisting and curling it into shape.

6 Dust with foliage, edelweiss and forest green. Tape the leaves around the base of the flower. Dust the base and tips of the leaves and the base of the stem with aubergine. Spray with edible spray varnish.

MATERIALS
White and pale green flowerpaste
28-, 33- and 35-gauge white wires
Forest, foliage, edelweiss, plum, aubergine and African violet petal dusts
White floristry tape
Edible spray varnish (Fabilo)

EQUIPMENT
Non-stick board
Silk veining ceramic tool (HP)
Dusting brushes
Scissors
Stargazer B petal veiner

Golden spider lily

This Chinese species – Lycoris aurea – is one of about 20 species of spider lily that produce beautifully fragile flowers that help to add impact to any floral arrangement. There are also other species that have white, orange, pink or red flowers.

MATERIALS
26-, 28- and 30-gauge white wires
Pale yellow and green flowerpaste
Daffodil, sunflower, African violet, aubergine, coral, vine green and foliage petal dusts
Nile green floristry tape
Clear alcohol

EQUIPMENT
Wire cutters
Dusting brushes
Non-stick board
Stargazer B petal veiner (SKGI)
Dresden tool (Jem)
Plain-edge cutting wheel
Fine-nose pliers

PISTIL

1 Take a half length of 30-gauge wire and blend a small ball of yellow paste onto the wire about 5 cm (2 in) from the tip. Work the paste to the tip to create a fine, smooth pistil. Flatten the tip slightly by pinching with your finger and thumb and flattening with another finger. Curve gracefully. Dust the pistil with a touch of vine green at the tip and a mixture of daffodil and sunflower from the base fading towards the tip.

STAMENS

2 Repeat the above process to create the stamens – they should be very slightly shorter than the pistil and do not flatten their tips. Next, add a tiny sausage shape pointed at both ends, to the tip. (As with other fine stamens of this nature I prefer to use cold porcelain, making the final result much stronger.) Make six more.

3 Curve the length of the stamens to follow the line of the pistil. Dust the length of the stamens as for the pistil. Colour the tips yellow with African violet and aubergine. Tape the six stamens around the pistil using quarter-width nile green floristry tape.

PETALS

4 Use 28-gauge white wires for the petals. Roll a ball of yellow paste onto the wire to create a slightly shorter length but with more bulk than the stamens. Flatten the shape against the non-stick board using the flat side of the stargazer B petal veiner. Texture the surface using the stargazer B veiner, pressing firmly to leave fine veining.

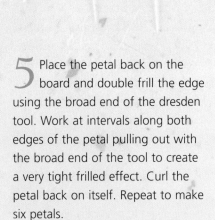

5 Place the petal back on the board and double frill the edge using the broad end of the dresden tool. Work at intervals along both edges of the petal pulling out with the broad end of the tool to create a very tight frilled effect. Curl the petal back on itself. Repeat to make six petals.

COLOURING AND ASSEMBLY

6 It is up to you if you dust now or when the flower is taped together. I prefer to wire the petals around the stamens first using half-width nile green tape and then colour. This allows me to create a more balanced finish between the petals. Tape three petals on first and then position the other three slightly behind and in between the joins. It helps at this stage if the petals are still pliable as you will be able to create more interesting curls.

7 Add a ball of yellow paste at the back of the flower and work it to create an elongated neck shape. Use the broad end of the dresden tool with a touch of clear alcohol to try and blend the paste into the base of the petals.

8 Dust the flower using a mixture of daffodil and sunflower. Add tinges of coral to the edges.

OVARY

9 Add a ball of green paste at the base of the flower to represent the ovary. Divide into three sections using the plain-edge cutting wheel. Pinch each section between your finger and thumb. Dust with foliage and vine green.

BUDS

10 Bend a hook in the end of a third of a length of 26-gauge wire. Form a cone-shaped bud using pale yellow paste. Insert the hooked wire into about half the length of the bud and then work the base of the bud down onto the wire to elongate its shape. Divide the length into three using the plain-edge cutting wheel. Dust as for the flower and add an ovary.

Wire vine

This delicate trailing foliage has a very complicated Latin name for such a small leaf - Muehlenbeckia axillaris! Its common names are just as much fun - maindenhair vine, creeping wire vine and my favourite, the mattress vine! Although the plant has a very small leaf it both builds structure within a bouquet and softens a design at the same time.

MATERIALS

26-, 28-, 33- and 35-gauge white wires
Pale green flowerpaste
Nile green floristry tape
Foliage, forest and aubergine petal dusts
Edible spray varnish (Fabilo)

EQUIPMENT

Wire cutters
Non-stick board
Small rose leaf veiner or large briar rose
    leaf veiner (SKGI)
Fine curved scissors
Small ball tool
Flat dusting brushes

LEAVES

1 Cut several lengths of 33- or 35-gauge wire into very short lengths. Blend a tiny ball of pale green paste onto the end of a dry wire. Work the ball between your finger and thumb to create a slight point at both ends.

2 Place the shape against the non-stick board and using the flat side of a leaf veiner simply flatten, or as I prefer to call it, 'splat', the shape to thin it out and form the leaf shape. Remove the veiner and take a look at the form – it might need a trim here and there with fine scissors to keep a more uniform shape. However, with practice you will find that the 'splatted' shapes start to form a uniform shape of their own.

3 Soften the edges with a small ball tool and then vein using a tiny rose leaf veiner or use the tighter, smaller veined section of a larger briar rose leaf veiner. Remove the leaf from the veiner and pinch from the base to the tip. Repeat to create what will seem like a few million leaves. I suggest listening to some music while you work!

4 Tape the leaves onto a fine-gauge wire, gradually adding slightly stronger wires for support if needed. Use quarter-width nile green tape and alternate the leaves down the stem, starting with the smallest and gradually increasing in size.

COLOURING

5 Dust the upper surface of each leaf using a touch of forest green and overdust with foliage green. Add a tinge of aubergine around the edges and to the main trailing stem and short stems that might be visible too. Spray lightly with edible spray varnish.

Winterberry

Winterberry (Ilex verticillata) is a type of holly native to America and Canada. The plant loses its foliage during the autumn allowing these stunning berries to show themselves off to their full potential! The berries are mostly red but there are yellow and orange forms too.

MATERIALS
18-, 20-, 22-, 33- and 35-gauge wires
Red, yellow or orange flowerpaste (depending on colour of berries you want to make)
Ruby, red, tangerine, aubergine, sunflower, nutkin brown and foliage petal dusts
Edible spray varnish or full glaze
Brown floristry tape

EQUIPMENT
Wire cutters
Fine-nose pliers
Tealight
Cigarette lighter or matches
Flat dusting brushes

BERRIES

1 Cut several lengths of 35- or 33-gauge wire into very short lengths. Take several wires at a time, line up the ends and then bend them all in one go with a pair of fine-nose pliers.

2 Light the tealight and burn the hooked end of the wires. This will leave them looking black.

3 Roll balls of your chosen colour of flowerpaste. Moisten the hook and push a single wire into each berry. Leave to firm up a little before the next stage.

COLOURING AND ASSEMBLY

4 Dust the berries to create the desired effect. I use red, ruby and a tinge of aubergine for the very red forms; tangerine and red for the orange varieties; and sunflower and tangerine for the yellow. Allow to dry, then spray with edible spray varnish or dip into a full glaze. You might need a few layers of glaze to create very shiny berries. Allow to dry. Dust the short stems with foliage and aubergine petal dusts.

5 Tape over a short length of 22-gauge wire with half-width brown tape to create a twig effect. Tape the berries quite tightly onto the twig. To create a larger piece, tape several smaller twigs onto a 20- or 18-gauge wire. I mostly use short twigs in a spray of flowers. Dust over the twigs with nutkin brown petal dust.

SPRAYS &
ARRANGEMENTS

Crescent spray

This style of spray is very useful for filling space and also for following a curve on a cake. It was the first shaped spray I was taught when I started making sugar flowers.

SPRAYS & ARRANGEMENTS

FLOWERS

9 stephanotis flowers (see page 39)
7 stephanotis buds (see page 39)
2 fully open yellow gardenias
   (see page 40–3)
1 full gardenia (see pages 40–3)
3 half gardenias (see pages 40–3)
1 gardenia bud (see page 40)
7 stems of smilax (see page 46)
6 stems of lily of the valley (see page 38)
7 stems of wire vine (see page 84)

EQUIPMENT

22- and 24-gauge wires
Wire cutters
Fine-nose pliers
Nile green floristry tape

PREPARATION

1 Strengthen any stems that require extra support or length using an appropriate gauge wire and half-width nile green floristry tape.

ASSEMBLY

2 You need to form two 'arms' for this spray. Create a line/arm using two stephanotis buds and three flowers. Add the elements to a 22-gauge wire with half-width nile green tape. Alternate the buds and flowers down the wire. Repeat to create a mirror image and then bend both stems to a 90-degree angle and tape them together. This forms the base of the spray and also the handle that will be inserted into the posy pick. Trim off any excess wires as you work to cut down on some of the bulk.

3 Add another shorter stem of stephanotis to create the width of the spray. This helps to balance out the overall shape.

4 Place the largest gardenia flower in the centre of the spray to create the focal point. This flower should stand higher than any of the others in the spray. Continue to add the remaining gardenia flowers and buds around the focal flower to fill out more of the shape of the spray. Use the small flowers towards the edges.

2

3

4

5 Add the ruscus foliage around the edges of the spray and use the gardenia leaves behind the focal flower and some around the base of the spray too. These will help to hide any 'holes' in the display.

6 Use the lily of the valley stems to soften the edges of the spray. Group the flowers and use them at opposite ends of the display.

7 Add the trailing stems of wire vine to create a more relaxed feel to the spray. Trim off any excess wires and tape over the handle of the spray with full-width nile green tape to neaten it.

Circle game

A garland can work well as a table decoration or wall hanging after the flowers have been used on a cake. Here I have used a twisted twig garland decorated with the flowers from the Cosmos cake on pages 112–3.

FLOWERS

2 pink cosmos flowers, plus 3 buds and
   foliage (see pages 60–2)
4 zinnia flowers, plus foliage
   (see pages 63–5)
6 groups of cotinus foliage (see page 47)
25 ornamental grasses (see page 73)

EQUIPMENT

24- and 22-gauge wires
Nile green floristry tape
Fine-nose pliers
Wire cutters
Sharp scissors
Twisted twig garland
Brown paper-covered reel wire
Broad gold organza ribbon

PREPARATION

1 Use 24- or 22-gauge wires and half-width nile green floristry tape to strengthen any of the flowers or foliage that need extra support.

ASSEMBLY

2 Group together a single cosmos flower and three zinnia flowers using half-width nile green floristry tape. Reserve the fourth zinnia for the smaller spray. Trim off any excess wires at this stage to cut down on some of the bulk. Add the cotinus foliage to fill in the gaps in the spray. Try to keep the foliage tight so that there are no large areas where you can see through the spray. Add some of the zinnia foliage too.

3 Use the fine cosmos buds and leaves and the ornamental grasses around the edges of the spray to soften the overall effect. Trim off the excess wires and tape over the stem again to tidy it up.

4 Tie the spray onto the twisted twig garland using a couple of lengths of brown paper covered wire. Feed the wire through the spray and tighten it around the garland to hold it in place. Trim off the excess wire. Repeat using the remaining cosmos, zinnia, grasses and foliage to add a smaller spray at the opposite side of the garland. Add a trail and bow of gold organza ribbon.

1

2

3

Between the lines

My friend Fumi gave me this very fragile Japanese black basket a while ago. The black lines of the basket provide a wonderful framework for arrangements of brightly coloured flowers. It is important when arranging flowers to create lines of colour or texture running through the work to link the components together.

2

3

FLOWERS
3 stems of sandersonia (see pages 50–1)
2 full-blown roses (see pages 52–4)
1 rosebud (see pages 18–21)
3 hosta leaves (see page 29)
3 beetleweed leaves (see page 72)
3 bromeliad leaves (see page 80)
3 stems of yellow ginger lily
　(see pages 48–9)

EQUIPMENT
18-, 20- and 22-gauge wires
Nile green floristry tape
Wire cutters or sharp scissors
Black Japanese basket
Florists' staysoft
Fine-nose pliers

PREPARATION

1 Add strength or length to the various flower stems if they require it by taping them on to a stronger wire using half-width nile green floristry tape – the gauge number will depend upon the weight of the flower. Place a ball of staysoft into the base of the basket.

ASSEMBLY

2 Bend a hook in the end of each stem of sandersonia – this will help to hold and steady these long stems in the staysoft. Use two long stems to create an 'S' shape flowing through the centre of the basket. Place a third shorter stem to the left of the arrangement to balance the design. Bend the tips of each stem to exaggerate and define the curved lines.

3 Add the large full-blown rose at the centre of the arrangement to create the focal point. Use the other rose and rosebud to create a line of colour through the centre of the arrangement.

4 Use the hosta, beetleweed and bromeliad leaves to frame the focal area and to add depth and layers to the arrangement. Fine-nose pliers are useful at this stage to help push the wires into the staysoft.

5 Finally, add the yellow ginger lilies to fill in the remaining space and add a bit more movement.

Metallica

A metallic extended trail of wire and mesh form the basic structure and line of this unusual and very modern bridal bouquet design.

FLOWERS

1 pale pink large rose (see pages 18–21)
1 pale pink half rose (see pages 18–21)
2 stems of Egyptian fan orchids
 (see page 55)
1 green spider chrysanthemum
 (see pages 34–5)
20 stems of pink ornamental grass
 (see page 73)
5 eyelash orchids (see pages 56–7)
7 begonia leaves, assorted sizes
 (see page 28)
5 stephanotis (see page 39)
5 stems of wire vine (see page 84)
3 stems of trailing succulents
 (see page 45)

EQUIPMENT

20- and 22-gauge wire
Nile green floristry tape
Wire cutters and sharp scissors
Florists' silver wire
Fine-nose pliers
Florists' mesh wire
Heavy glass vase

PREPARATION

1 Strengthen any flower or foliage stems that need extra support by taping 20- or 22-gauge wire into the main stems using quarter-width or half-width nile green floristry tape. The gauge of wire will depend on the weight of each item.

ASSEMBLY

2 Bend two lengths of florists' silver wire to a 90-degree angle using fine-nose pliers. Trim off any excess using sharp scissors or wire cutters. Tape the stems together using full-width nile green floristry tape. Add the full rose to create the focal point of the bouquet – this flower needs to stand higher in the bouquet than any others. Tape in a half rose by the side of the full rose. Frame the full rose using the two stems of fan orchids. Start to create twists and turns to the lengths of florists' wire to add more dimension to the work.

3 Continue to frame the focal rose using the spider chrysanthemum towards the back of the bouquet and then group the grasses at the base. Place the eyelash orchids together to fill in the remaining space.

4 Use the begonia leaves in an overlapping formation behind the flowers to help define the shape of the bouquet a little more. Put in the stephanotis flowers and a smaller begonia leaf to gradually work down towards the tip of the bouquet.

5 Add two trails of florists' mesh winding them around the existing trails of silver wire and then finally weave the stems of wire vine and trailing succulents through the wire and mesh and around the top section of the bouquet to soften the edges.

6 Place a twist of florists' mesh inside the glass vase to help support the bouquet.

1

2

3

Silver trail posy

Although in theory a posy of flowers is fairly easy to assemble, you will find that you use quite a lot of flowers to complete a project of this sort. A balanced result is needed to help form the characteristic posy shape. I have updated the style slightly by adding a cage and trails of fine crimped metallic wires that catch the light.

FLOWERS

1 green-tinged large full rose
   (see pages 18–21)
6 hydrangea florets (see pages 69–71)
3 Christmas orchids (see pages 25–7)
3 masdevallia orchids (see page 79)
3 blue butterfly bush flowers
   (see page 78)
8 beetleweed leaves (see page 72)

EQUIPMENT

Nile green floristry tape
24- and 28-gauge wires
Double-sided pink/green satin ribbon
Fine-nose pliers
Wire cutters
Fine silver, pale green and turquoise
   metallic crimped reel wires
Pale aqua beaded wires

PREPARATION

1 Use half-width nile green tape and 24-gauge wire to strengthen or lengthen any of the flower stems that need it.

2 This posy is built on a series of figure-of-eight ribbon loops – these are optional but can prove useful for filling in gaps in a posy or even at the heart of a crescent-shaped spray (see pages 88–9). Simply form figure-of-eight double loops. The double-sided ribbon works well for this purpose. Bend a length of 28-gauge wire at the centre of the loops and twist it together to hold the ribbon in place. Repeat this process as required and then layer up the loops to form a circle of ribbons on which the posy can be built.

ASSEMBLY

3 Use the full rose as the centre and focal point of the posy – this flower should stand higher than any others. Tape into place using half-width nile green tape.

4 Start to encircle the rose with the hydrangea florets. Trim away excess bulk wires from the handle of the spray as you work.

5 Continue to work around the posy adding the Christmas and masdevallia orchids, alternating them as you build the arrangement.

6 Create a little more interest by adding cool notes of blue clerodendron flowers evenly around the posy.

7 Use the beetleweed leaves as the final layer of the posy to create a more compact feel and to frame the display. Finally, weave around the flowers with silver, pale green and turquoise crimped wires and curls of aqua-coloured beaded wire. Add trails of crimped wire to soften the whole display.

1

3

5

Gothica

Several years ago I was involved with a group of fellow enthusiasts who created a display table of floral footwear for a craft exhibition. It was during this period that I started to introduce paper-covered wire curls and plaits into my work and so it seemed a natural choice to use this weaved technique to build up the base to my fantasy shoe.

FLOWERS
2 Egyptian fan orchids (see page 55)
5 begonia leaves (see page 28)
1 full-blown rose, plus one set of rose
   leaves (see pages 52–4)
5 stems of trailing succulents
   (see page 45)

EQUIPMENT
Sole template (see page 142)
Sharp scissors
Fine artists' mesh
18-gauge wires
Nile green floristry tape
Wire cutters
Green paper-covered reel
Fine-nose pliers
Cold porcelain (see pages 13–4)
Fine crimped metallic wires
Fine ribbon or braid (optional)
Fabric or fine glass beads, to line the shoe
Non-toxic hi-tack craft glue (Impex)
Florists' staysoft

PREPARATION

1 Use a sharp pair of scissors to carefully cut out the sole shape from fine artists' mesh. Bend and curve the mesh to form the arched sole shape.

2 Tape three 18-gauge wires together with full-width nile green floristry tape to act as the base for the heel. Leave the wires free at both ends to help to create the curved heal shape. Hook the wires at one end through the mesh sole. Use craft glue and layers of cold porcelain to help bond the heel and sole together. Leave at least overnight to dry. Add extra layers of cold porcelain to cover the basic form of the heel and a thin layer over the sole to cover the mesh. Again leave at least overnight to dry.

SHOE BUILD-UP

3 Use lengths of green paper covered wire to wrap around the basic heel structure. Increase the wire around the base and at the top of the heel to emphasize the shape. Gradually start to twist and pull up lengths of wire to form the top section of the shoe and then twist them together to form the extreme point at the back of the shoe.

4 Weave twists and curls to form interesting shapes within the sides of the shoe. Continue to work the design of the shoe in a similar way throughout. Try to build up strength in the shoe as you work, increasing the amount of weaving in certain areas. Keep checking that the shoe is steady when placed on to a flat surface.

5 Add extra weaved sections using fine crimped metallic wires. Small amounts of ribbon and braid can also be used at this stage too if desired.

6 The inside of the shoe can be lined at this stage with fabric or textured cold porcelain or simply painted lightly with non-toxic hi-tack craft glue and covered with tiny glass beads. Allow to dry overnight.

ASSEMBLY

7 Attach small amounts of florists' staysoft into the toe of the shoe and at the heel area. Use fine-nose pliers to hook the end of each flower stem. This will add extra support to the flowers and help hold them in place. Start the arrangement using the two fan orchids and the begonia leaves. Use the full-blown rose as the focal flower of the display. Finally, add trails of succulents around the heel and through holes in the weaved sides of the shoe. Use the pliers to help push the stems into difficult tight areas.

Anemone arrangement

I love using purple and red together. Here the purple anemone works well with the red beetleweed leaves and red-tinged grasses. The slender black vase and tray create a very dramatic, eye-catching decoration that could be used with a small cake or around the home – especially if made with cold porcelain rather than flowerpaste.

FLOWERS

Large spray

1 anemone (see pages 66–8)

5 begonia leaves (see page 28)

3 red beetleweed leaves (see page 72)

5 hydrangea flowers (see pages 69–71)

2 groups of tillandsia foliage
  (see page 81)

3 bromeliad leaves (see page 80)

5 stems of lily of the valley (see page 38)

20 ornamental grasses (see page 73)

Small spray

1 anemone bud (see pages 66–8)

1 begonia leaf (see page 28)

1 hydrangea flower (see pages 69–71)

7 ornamental grasses (see page 73)

EQUIPMENT

22- and 24-gauge wires

Wire cutters

Fine-nose pliers

Nile green floristry tape

Narrow black bamboo vase

Black ceramic tray

PREPARATION

1 Depending upon the support needed for each flower or leaf, tape a 24- or 22-gauge wire onto the existing stems with half-width nile green floristry tape.

2

3

ASSEMBLY

2 Use the anemone flower as the starting point, and the focal point, for the large spray. Add the begonia and beetleweed leaves around the flower using half-width tape. Keep the flower high in the centre of the spray and tuck the beetleweed foliage tight in behind it.

3 Tuck in the hydrangea flowers evenly around the anemone. Add the tillandsia foliage group to the left-hand side of the spray. Extend the length and balance it with the bromeliad leaves. Trim off any excess wires as you work.

4 Group and pull in the lily of the valley stems at the front of the spray and balance it with another stem or two to the left-hand side of the spray in amongst the tillandsia leaves. Use the grasses in groups around the spray to extend the length and soften the edges of the display.

5 Place the handle of the spray into the narrow vase and display on top of the black ceramic tray, accompanied by a small, corsage-style spray.

Red rose arrangement

A single red rose is the focal point of this luscious bouquet of rich red holly berries and autumnal beetleweed leaves. Twines of gold paper-covered wire and the delicate foliage of the wire vine soften and define the shape of the spray, which is suitable for a wedding, engagement or Valentine, or even as a Christmas cake decoration.

FLOWERS

1 large red rose and one bud
  (see pages 18–21)
3 stems of winterberry (see page 85)
10 red beetleweed leaves (see page 72)
5 trailing stems of wire vine (see page 84)
A few dogwood berries (see page 118)

EQUIPMENT

20- and 22-gauge wires
Wire cutters
Fine-nose pliers
Nile green floristry tape
Tape shredder or scissors
Gold paper-covered wire
Red beaded wire
Silver napkin ring, to display (optional)

PREPARATION

1 Add extra wire to the floral components as needed by taping them onto extra lengths of 22- or 20-gauge wires using half-width nile green floristry tape. A tape shredder can speed up this process or the tape can be cut carefully by hand using a pair of scissors.

ASSEMBLY

2 Use the red rose as the focal point of the spray and tape three stems of berried holly around it. Trim off the excess wire as you work to cut down any bulk that might build up.

3 Add both the flat and curled beetleweed leaves to fill in the gaps to create the outline of the spray and to add more tapered length. Next, add the rose bud and dogwood berries around the central rose.

4 Add the trailing stems of the wire vine to add interest to the edges of the spray. Use the longest length to add to the total length.

5 Use lengths of gold paper-covered wire to create a curly effect and added length to the spray. Tape in smaller curly lengths of red beaded wire to complement the luscious red berries. Display in a vase or as shown here in a silver napkin ring.

2

3

4

French connection

This beautiful arrangement was created by one of my students, Christiane, after a class I had given on spider chrysanthemums. Christian created this exquisite arrangement over a number of days. She entered it into a sugarcraft competition, winning a gold trophy for it. She kindly allowed me to borrow her piece to be photographed for this book. The perspex base is actually a wine-bottle stand that she bought from a charity shop. It conveniently had a hole in the middle, making it ideal for a flower arrangement!

FLOWERS

Assorted berries, flowers, foliage and
  succulents
1 green spider chrysanthemum,
  plus leaves (see pages 34–5)

EQUIPMENT

18-, 20- and 22-gauge wires
Wire cutters
Nile green floristry tape
Perspex wine-bottle stand or similar
Green florists' staysoft
Fine-nose pliers
    Dried Spanish moss

PREPARATION

1 Strengthen any of the flower
and foliage stems that require
extra length or support using an
appropriate gauge of wire and half-
width nile green floristry tape.

ASSEMBLY

2 Fill the hole in the stand with
green florists' staysoft. Use the
assorted stems of berries, flowers,
foliage and succulents to create a long
arched line through the arrangement.
A hook in the end of each flower
stem will help to give more support.

3 Add the spider chrysanthemum
to create the focal point of the
arrangement. Fill in around the flower
with chrysanthemum leaves and
succulents. Hide any staysoft that
is visible with dried Spanish moss.

Ruby rose bouquet

This bouquet was created by me and four friends for our friend Eileen's 65th birthday cake. The flowers were used next to a chocolate ganache-coated cake. My partners in crime were Alice, Jan, Ann and last but not least as she baked the cake too – Alex!

FLOWERS

1 large rose, 3 half roses and 1 rosebud
   (see pages 18–21)
5 hydrangea flowers (see pages 69–71)
20 brunia seed-heads (see page 76)
20 large pink ornamental grasses
   (see page 73)
9 stems of trailing succulents
   (see page 45)
2 stems of Geraldton waxplant
   (see page 77)

EQUIPMENT

20- and 22-gauge wires
Nile green floristry tape
Gold, pink and burgundy paper-covered
   reel wires
Wire cutters
Fine-nose pliers
Glass vase

PREPARATION

1 Tape a 20- or 22-gauge wire onto any of the flower or foliage stems that require extra support or length.

2 Take a long length of each of the different coloured paper-covered wires and twist them together very loosely. Form a large heart shape using the paper-covered wires, bending the top curve of the heart down to form a handle for the bouquet. Twist the point of the heart together and then create a curl in the end of each wire.

ASSEMBLY

3 Pull in the full rose as the focal flower. Add the half roses and rosebud around the full rose and secure to the handle created by the heart framework with half-width nile green floristry tape. Add the hydrangea flowers to fill in the large gaps between the roses.

4 Group together the brunia seed-heads to pack out the sides of the bouquet. Tape them into the bouquet a few groups at a time.

5 Use the grasses, trailing succulents and wax flowers around the edges of the bouquet to soften the feel and add more detailed interest.

6 I used paper-covered wire twisted around the handle of the bouquet to hide the mechanics when it was used next to the chocolate cake. Here the bouquet is simply displayed in a glass vase.

Tangerine dream

This bouquet was made by my friend Sathya, using techniques that I had taught her over the last couple of years. She won a gold award in the floral class at the Hotel Olympia Salon Culinaire for this beautiful piece of work.

FLOWERS

30 beetleweed leaves (see page 72) and
    12–15 assorted decorative leaves
3 orange roses (see pages 18–21)
1 stem of sandersonia (see pages 50–1)
3 golden spider lilies (see pages 82–3)
3 poppy seed-heads (see page 37)
2 stems of orange Christmas orchids
    (see pages 25–7)

EQUIPMENT

20- and 22-gauge wires
Nile green floristry tape
Fine-nose pliers
Wire cutters
Orange, aubergine and soft green
    paper-covered reel wire
Glass vase

PREPARATION

1 Use 22- or 20-gauge wire, depending upon the weight of the flower, to support or elongate any of the flowers or foliage that require it.

2 Take several lengths of orange, aubergine and soft green paper-covered wire and twist the ends together. At this stage a spare pair of hands or at least a hook or a clamp will make the next job of plaiting the lengths of paper-covered wire together much easier. Create either one very

long plait or two slightly shorter ones to complete the trail and curl through the bouquet. Do not try to be too neat with this process, it tends to look better with a more random feel.

ASSEMBLY

3 Thread several beetleweed leaves into the plait at intervals, gradually increasing them in size. The stem wires can be hidden amongst the soft green paper-covered wires – just make sure that they are secured well to stop them falling out at a later stage.

4 Create a curl at the other end of the plait and then pull in the three roses. As a guideline, the focal point should be approximately two-thirds from the tip of the bouquet with another third to the top. Tape the roses in with half- or even full-width floristry tape to keep them very secure. Add a few of the larger, flatter beetleweed leaves around the roses.

5 Add the croton foliage to surround the roses – these can be taped in singularly or in groups – whichever feels more comfortable. This is a large bouquet and can be

heavy to work with, so don't rush the process. Add the stem of sandersonia to trail the length of the bouquet.

6 Tape in the three very fragile golden spider lilies, taking extreme care. Space these flowers evenly around the bouquet. Pull in the poppy seed-heads at this stage too – keep them grouped at the right-hand side of the bouquet.

7 Finally, add the orange orchid stems. Their buds will help to soften the edges of the bouquet.

8 The back of the bouquet can be completed using a ring of beetleweed leaves to hide the mechanics at the back. The handle can be wrapped with ribbon or, as shown here, using another finer plait of paper-covered wire. The handle of the bouquet should be of a size that is easy for a bride to carry, but if you are planning to insert the handle into a large posy pick to insert into a cake then you will need to trim off the excess wires as you work to keep the bulk to a minimum. Display the bouquet in a suitable vase or container.

4

CAKES

Cosmos cake

This pink, iced two-tier wedding cake is adorned with a refreshing combination of pink cosmos and vibrant zinnia blooms. The ornamental grasses help to soften the edges of the sprays and also add an almost rustic quality to the cake design – ideal for a more informal setting.

MATERIALS

13-cm (5-in) and 20-cm (8-in) round rich
  fruitcakes
Apricot glaze
1kg (2 lb) white almond paste
Icing sugar
1.4 kg (3 lb) white sugarpaste, to cover
  cake and board
Ruby paste food colour
Clear alcohol (Cointreau or kirsch)
Fine pink satin ribbon, to trim the cakes
Bright pink velvet ribbon, to trim the
  baseboard
Non-toxic glue stick

EQUIPMENT

13-cm (5-in) and 20-cm (8-in) round thin
  cake cards
Pastry brush
Rolling pin
Sugarpaste smoothers
Make-up sponge
35-cm (14-in) round cake drum
Floral embosser
Posy pick

FLOWERS

2 pink cosmos flowers, plus buds and
  foliage (see pages 60–2)
5 orange zinnias (see pages 63–5)
25 ornamental grasses (see page 73)
5 sprigs of cotinus foliage (see page 47)

PREPARATION

1 Place each cake onto the thin cake cards of the same size. Brush both cakes with warmed apricot glaze. Roll out the almond paste on a light dusting of icing sugar. Polish the surface of the paste with a round-edged sugarpaste smoother to even out any unevenness in the rolled paste. Cover each cake in turn. Trim off the excess paste and polish the top of the cake with the round-edged smoother and the sides with the straight-edged smoother to achieve a neat finish. Allow to dry for a couple of days if time allows.

2 Colour the sugarpaste with a little ruby paste food colour. Knead the paste to distribute the colour evenly; be careful not to knead in too many air bubbles into the icing. Allow the paste to rest for a few hours.

3 Moisten the surface of the cake with clear alcohol using a make-up sponge. Roll out the sugarpaste and cover the cake as described above in step 1. An extra polished finish may be achieved by pressing a pad of sugarpaste into your palm and using it to work quickly over the surface. This will also help to soften any cracks in the icing, although cracked edges usually indicate that the sugarpaste has not been kneaded enough.

4 Cover the cake drum with the coloured sugarpaste. Trim off the excess and smooth as for the cake. Position the larger cake centrally on top of the coated board. Use the straight-edged smoother to create a tight, neat join at the base of the cake. Place the smaller cake on top and repeat to create a neat join.

5 Emboss a floral design at intervals around the board edge. Allow the coating to dry for about a day or two if you have time. Attach a fine band of pink ribbon around the base of the two cakes using a small amount of softened sugarpaste/clear alcohol to secure the ribbon in place. Attach a band of bright pink velvet ribbon to the board edge using the non-toxic glue stick.

FLOWERS

6 Wire together two informal sprays, one large and one small (see pages 90–1). Insert a plastic posy pick into the top tier and then place the handle of the spray into it. Rearrange the grasses if needed to create a more relaxed design. Add the small corsage at the base of the cake.

White wedding

A bouquet of stephanotis flowers used en masse creates a very elegant and graceful display on this single-tier wedding cake. Once mastered, stephanotis can be produced fairly quickly, making them a useful addition to both the novice and more experienced flower maker's repertoire.

MATERIALS
25-cm (10-in) oval fruitcake
Apricot glaze
Icing sugar
1.25 kg (2 lb 10 oz) white almond paste
Clear alcohol (Cointreau or kirsch)
2 kg (4½ lb) white sugarpaste, to cover the cake and larger board
White royal icing
Gold pearl sugar dragées
White satin ribbon, to trim the board
Non-toxic glue stick (Pritt) or corsage pins
Nile green floristry tape

EQUIPMENT
25-cm (10-in) oval thin cake board
Pastry brush
Large non-stick rolling pin
Make-up sponge
Sugarpaste smoothers
38-cm (15-in) oval thin cake board
Sharp knife
Piping bag and no. 42 piping tube
Nile green floristry tape
Fine-nose pliers
Wire cutters
Pearl effect beads
Green crimped reel wire
Gold paper-covered reel wire

FLOWERS
40–50 stephanotis flowers (see page 39)
10 beetleweed leaves (see page 72)
2 groups of tillandsia foliage (see page 81)
9 stems of trailing succulent, two of which sprayed gold (see page 45)
5 stems of wire vine (see page 84)

PREPARATION

1 Place the cake on to the board of the same size. Brush the cake with warmed apricot glaze and cover with white almond paste. If time allows, leave the cake to dry overnight. Moisten the surface of the almond paste with clear alcohol using a make-up sponge. Cover the cake with sugarpaste and use the sugarpaste smoothers to create a neat finish.

2 Lightly moisten and then cover the larger oval board with sugarpaste. Trim off the excess with a sharp knife. Place the cake in the centre of the covered board. Blend the join between the base of the cake and the board using the straight-edged sugarpaste smoother. Leave the sugarpaste to firm up for a few hours or overnight.

3 Pipe a royal-icing shell border around the base of the cake using the piping bag fitted with a no. 42 piping tube. While the shells are still wet quickly add gold pearl dragées at intervals around the base. Allow to dry.

4 Attach a band of white satin ribbon to the edge of the board using a non-toxic glue stick (or corsage pins) to hold it in place.

ASSEMBLY

5 Gather and tape together the stephanotis flowers a few at a time to create the central posy shape and then encircle the flowers with beetleweed leaves. Next, add the tillandsia leaves into the posy, positioning them opposite each other and gradually add trails of succulents and wire vine, making sure you sweep some of the trailing stems around the top curve of the posy.

6 Weave a gold paper-covered wire
nest around the posy section of
the bouquet and also to create trails
that tangle amongst the foliage.
Introduce succulents that have been
sprayed gold and also pull in lengths
of wired pearl-like beads using green
crimped wire to tangle as you work.
Tape over the handle of the bouquet
with full-width nile green tape.
Wrap the handle of the
bouquet either with gold
paper-covered wire or
ribbon.

Crowning glory

*This spectacular cake looks rather like a decorative hat!
The lengths of yellow, green and aubergine paper-covered wire
help to frame the cake and add a little drama to the design too.*

MATERIALS

20-cm (8-in) curved leaf-shaped fruitcake
Apricot glaze
Icing sugar
750 g (1 lb 10 oz) white almond paste
Clear alcohol (Cointreau or kirsch)
750 g (1 lb 10 oz) champagne sugarpaste
Lemon yellow velvet ribbon, to trim
    the cake
Royal icing
Flowerpaste
Edible gold leaf
Cocoa butter
Ruby, aubergine, vine and foliage petal
    dusts
Nile green floristry tape
Yellow, green and aubergine paper-
    covered wires

EQUIPMENT

20-cm (8-in) curved leaf cake board
Pastry brush
Large non-stick rolling pin
Make-up sponge
Sugarpaste smoothers
Non-stick board
Small non-stick rolling pin
Sharp knife
Pin oak leaf paper punch
Mug and saucer
Fine paintbrushes
Posy pick

FLOWERS

3 sandersonia flowers (see pages 50–1)
3 golden gardenias (see page 44)
5 groups of cotinus foliage (see page 47)
2 stems of spider orchid (see page 58)
1 golden spider lily (see pages 82–3)
10 ornamental grasses (see page 73)

PREPARATION

1 Place the cake onto the cake board. Brush the cake with warmed apricot glaze and cover with white almond paste. Leave to dry overnight. Use a make-up sponge to moisten the almond paste with clear alcohol and then cover with champagne sugarpaste. Use sugarpaste smoothers to create a smooth surface, particularly around the base of the cake. Allow to dry overnight.

2 Attach a band of yellow velvet ribbon around the base of the cake using a little royal icing (or sugarpaste softened to a similar consistency with clear alcohol).

DESIGN DETAIL

3 Roll out a small amount of well-kneaded flowerpaste on a non-stick board. Carefully open up a book of gold leaf. Peel the flowerpaste off the board to reveal its sticky side and then quickly lower the paste on top of the sheet of gold leaf. Gently rub the paste against the gold to bond the two together. Turn the paste over to reveal the coated side. Leave for 5 minutes or so to firm up slightly.

4 Trim off any excess white around the edges of the gold-coated flowerpaste with a sharp knife. Slide the paste into the leaf paper punch and cut out several leaf shapes. Attach the leaves onto the surface of the cake using a small amount of clear alcohol.

5 Place a small amount of grated cocoa butter on to a saucer and place over a mug of just boiled water to melt it. Add a little ruby petal dust to some of the cocoa butter to make a paint to add small dots and leaves around the gold leaves. Add a little aubergine petal dust to darken the colour and continue to add more detail and depth to the design. Mix a smaller amount of cocoa butter with vine green and foliage petal dusts and add extra dots and central veins to each of the gold oak leaves.

6 Tape together the spray of flowers. Insert a posy pick into the cake and place the handle of the spray into it. Curl the lengths of paper-covered wire to sit underneath the bottom section of the cake and curl the top lengths to create an attractive arrangement.

ASSEMBLY

7 Group together the three golden gardenia flowers using one as the focal flower so it should stand slightly higher than the other two in the spray. Tape them together to form a line using half-width nile green floristry tape. Next add two stems of the spider orchids to form the start of the 'S'-shaped line through the spray.

8 Cut several lengths of aubergine, yellow and soft green paper-covered wire and add to the spray to accentuate the 'S' shape of the spray. Add the single spider lily and the cotinus foliage to fill in any gaps. Soften the edges with the ornamental grasses.

Valentine

Although this cake was made with St Valentine's Day in mind with its vivid red roses, glossy berries and red beetleweed foliage, it would also be suitable for many other winter celebrations.

MATERIALS

20-cm (8-in) trefoil-shaped rich fruitcake
Apricot glaze
Icing sugar
750 g (1 lb 10 oz) white almond paste
Clear alcohol (Cointreau or kirsch)
1 kg (2 lb) white sugarpaste, to cover
   board and cake
24-gauge wire
Fresh egg white
Ruby, foliage and aubergine petal dusts
Edible spray varnish
Broad red velvet ribbon, to trim the board
Non-toxic glue stick (Pritt) or corsage pins
Fine red ribbon, to trim the cake
Small amount of royal icing
Red beaded wire
Nile green floristry tape
Gold paper-covered wire

EQUIPMENT

Pastry brush
Rolling pin
Make-up sponge
Sugarpaste smoothers
30-cm (12-in) round cake board
Fine-nose pliers
Posy pick

FLOWERS

Red rose arrangement (see pages 102–3)

Small corsage

1 rosebud (see pages 18–21)
1 sprig of winterberries (see page 85)
1 curled beetleweed leaf (see page 72)
1 stem of wire vine (see page 84)

PREPARATION

1 Brush the cake with apricot glaze and cover with white almond paste. Leave to dry overnight. Moisten the surface of the almond paste with clear alcohol using a make-up sponge and cover with white sugarpaste. Use sugarpaste smoothers to create a neat finish. A ball of sugarpaste pressed into the palm is good for smoothing the difficult angles and curves of the trefoil-shaped cake.

2 Cover the round cake board with white sugarpaste and place the cake on top. Carefully blend the join between the cake and the board using the straight-edged smoother, trying not to catch the coated board as you work. Leave to dry overnight.

3 To make the dogwood berries, attach a ball of pale green paste to the end of a hooked 24-gauge wire. Next, roll lots of small balls of green paste and collect them in a small pot. Soften some more paste with fresh egg-white, smear over the wired ball and roll it into the pot of balls – they will be picked up by the sticky sugar surface. Press them against the large ball to neaten the shape. Insert a short length of stamen into each ball. Trim as required. Dust with ruby, foliage and aubergine petal dusts. Spray with edible spray varnish.

ASSEMBLY

4 Attach a band of red velvet ribbon to the edge of the board using a non-toxic glue stick or corsage pins. Secure a band of thin red ribbon to the base of the cake with dots of royal icing at each indent. Alternatively, wet the ribbon, wipe off the excess water and carefully position it around the base.

5 Create three tight curls of red beaded wire using a pair of fine-nose pliers. Attach the curls to the trefoil indents using a little royal icing to hold them in place.

6 Assemble the spray. Insert a posy pick into the top of the cake and place the handle of the spray into it. Tape together the small corsage and add a curl of gold paper-covered wire. Wrap the handle of the corsage with red beaded wire and position on top of the board. Readjust the gold paper-covered wires to form a pleasing shape.

Ruby rose

This stunning two-tier cake with its trailing dark ruby rose bouquet would be suitable as a wedding cake or a ruby anniversary cake.

MATERIALS

15-cm (6-in) oval dummy cake
Clear alcohol (kirsch or Cointreau)
Icing sugar
1.4 kg (3 lb) champagne sugarpaste, to cover cakes and boards
23-cm (9-in) heart-shaped rich fruitcake
Apricot glaze
1kg (2 lb) white almond paste
Soft green ribbon, to trim the cakes
Small amount of royal icing (optional)
Pink striped ribbon, to trim the oval board
Broad soft green ribbon to trim the baseboard
Non-toxic glue stick (Pritt) or corsage pins
Double-sided carpet tape, large corsage pins or non-slip grip mat
White flowerpaste or edible gold leaf
Non-toxic hi-tack craft glue (Impex)

EQUIPMENT

Pastry brush
Rolling pin
23-cm (9-in) thin oval board
35-cm (14-in) heart-shaped baseboard
Sugarpaste smoothers
Make-up sponge
Large tilted perspex stand (Celcakes)
Pin oak leaf paper punch

FLOWERS

Ruby rose bouquet (see pages 106–7)

PREPARATION

1 The tilted top tier could be a rich fruitcake however, I prefer not to take the risk of having a sliding cake situation so I use a polystyrene dummy cake. It also helps with displaying the flowers at a difficult angle. Moisten the oval dummy cake with clear alcohol and cover with a layer of sugarpaste. Cover the thin oval board and the large heart-shaped board with sugarpaste. Place the dummy cake onto the oval board. Use the smoothers at the bottom edge of the dummy to work the paste to blend with the coated board. Leave to dry.

2 Brush the heart-shaped fruit cake with warmed apricot glaze and cover with a layer of almond paste. Leave to dry overnight. Coat the surface with clear alcohol using a make-up sponge and cover with champagne sugarpaste. Transfer the cake to the heart-shaped board. Use smoothers to create a smooth neat finish.

ASSEMBLY

3 Attach a band of soft green ribbon to the base of both cakes using royal icing or softened sugarpaste. Attach a band of pink, striped ribbon to the edge of the oval board and a broad soft green ribbon to the edge of the heart-shaped board using non-toxic glue or corsage pins.

4 Place the heart-shaped cake in front of the tilted stand. Position the oval dummy cake on top using double-sided carpet tape, large corsage pins or a non-slip grip mat.

5 Create the ruby rose bouquet and insert it into the dummy cake. Rearrange the trails of paper-covered wire to create an attractive design to connect the cakes together.

6 Using a pin oak paper punch and the flowerpaste/gold leaf technique outlined on page 116, cut out several gold leaves. Allow them to set slightly and attach some of the leaves onto both cakes using clear alcohol or royal icing. Add more to the wires of the bouquet using a tiny amount of non-toxic hi-tack glue.

Butterfly cake

A single butterfly used at the base of this pretty heart-shaped celebration cake helps to balance the overall design.

MATERIALS

25-cm (10-in) heart-shaped fruitcake
Apricot glaze
Icing sugar, sifted
1.25 kg (2 lb 10 oz) white almond paste
2 kg (4½ lb) champagne sugarpaste,
   to cover cake and boards
Clear alcohol (kirsch or Cointreau)
Silk-effect ivory paper, to trim the cake
Small amount of royal icing
Lemon yellow paper-covered wire
Edible gold leaf
Vine, foliage, daffodil, sunflower,
   edelweiss and black petal dusts
Flowerpaste
26- and 30-gauge white wires
Fine stamens
Nile green floristry tape
Decorative green ribbon, to trim the board
Non-toxic glue stick (Pritt) or corsage pins
Posy pick

EQUIPMENT

25-cm (10-in) heart-shaped thin cake board
Pastry brush
Rolling pin
Make-up sponge
Sugarpaste smoothers
35-cm (14-in) heart-shaped thin cake board
Leaf paper punch
Fine paintbrush
Butterfly cutter (Jem)
Anemone petal veiner (ALDV)
Fine-nose pliers
Sharp scalpel
Dusting brushes

FLOWERS

Crescent spray (see pages 88–9)

PREPARATION

1 Place the cake onto the same size board. Brush the cake with warmed apricot glaze and cover with white almond paste. If time allows leave the cake to dry overnight. Roll out the sugarpaste. Moisten the surface of the almond paste with clear alcohol using a make-up sponge. Cover the cake with sugarpaste using the sugarpaste smoothers to create a neat finish.

2 Lightly moisten and then cover the larger heart-shaped board with a layer of sugarpaste and trim off the excess. Transfer the cake to sit centrally on top of it. Blend the join between the base of the cake and the board using the straight-edged sugarpaste smoother. Leave the sugarpaste to firm up for a few hours or even overnight.

3 Secure a length of silk-effect paper ribbon to the sides of the cake using royal icing or softened sugarpaste/alcohol mix to hold it in place. Fasten the lemon yellow paper-covered wire around the base of the cake.

4 Cut out several gold leaf cut-outs using the leaf paper punch (see page 116). Attach the gold cut-outs to the sides of the cake at intervals using a little clear alcohol. Dilute some foliage and vine green petal dusts and add delicate spotted trails to each cut-out design using a fine paintbrush.

BUTTERFLY

5 Use the butterfly cutter to cut out four wing sections from flowerpaste, leaving a thick ridge in each section. Wire each section onto a 30-gauge white wire. Soften the edges and vein with the anemone petal veiner. Pinch each section from the base to the tip and allow to firm up before painting.

6 To make the body, attach a ball of flowerpaste to a hooked 26-gauge wire. Add a smaller ball for its head and a carrot shape for the tail. Divide the head into two sections using a sharp scalpel and insert a stamen into each to represent the antennae. Texture the body to create a hairy effect using the scalpel. Leave to dry before painting with a diluted mixture of black petal dust and clear alcohol.

CAKES

7 Tape the wing sections onto the body using quarter-width nile green floristry tape. Dust the wings with vine green and a mixture of daffodil and sunflower petal dusts. Add fine painted detail using the diluted black petal dust. Add white highlights to the tips. When complete, position the butterfly at the point of the cake.

ASSEMBLY

8 Attach a band of decorative green ribbon to the edge of the board using a non-toxic glue stick or corsage pins to hold it in place.

9 Assemble the crescent spray. Insert a posy pick into the cake and place the handle of the spray into it. Adjust and curve the trailing stems of wire vine to create a more relaxed finished display.

Purple plumage

The rich purple petals of the anemone add a regal quality to this two-tier wedding cake. Begonia leaves frame the dominant flower while the grasses and tillandsia foliage help to soften the edges.

MATERIALS

13-cm (5-in) and 23-cm (9-in) round rich fruitcakes
Apricot glaze
Icing sugar
1.25 kg (2 lb 10 oz) white almond paste
1.4 kg (3 lb) white sugarpaste, to cover cakes and drum
Clear alcohol (Cointreau or kirsch)
Pale lilac ribbon, to trim the cakes and the cake drum
Royal icing
Gold and grey braid, to trim the cakes
Non-toxic glue stick (Pritt) (or large corsage pins)

EQUIPMENT

13-cm (5-in) and 23-cm (9-in) round thin cake boards
Pastry brush
Large non-stick rolling pin
Sugarpaste smoothers
35-cm (14-in) round cake drum
Make-up sponge
Posy pick

FLOWERS

Anemone arrangement
(see pages 100–01)

Small spray

1 anemone bud (see pages 66–8)
1 begonia leaf (see page 28)
1 hydrangea (see pages 69–71)
1 sprig of tillandsia (see page 81)
10 ornamental grasses (see page 73)

PREPARATION

1 Place the cakes on to the same-sized cake boards. Brush each cake with warmed apricot glaze. Cover the cakes (and their boards) with almond paste. Use a curved-edge smoother on the top of the cakes and the straight-edged smoother around the sides to create a neat, smooth finish. Leave overnight to dry.

2 Lightly moisten the cake drum and cover with a layer of white sugarpaste. Moisten the surface of the almond paste-coated cakes with clear alcohol using a make-up sponge. Cover both cakes with white sugarpaste. Use the smoothers to create a neat finish. Place the large cake on top of the cake drum. Blend the join between the two using a straight-edged smoother. Place the smaller cake on top and again use the smoother to blend the edges of the two cakes together.

3 Attach a band of dusky lilac ribbon around both cakes using a small amount of royal icing or softened sugarpaste to hold it in place. Layer the ribbon with a length of gold and grey braid. Glue or pin a length of dusky lilac ribbon to the drum edge.

FLOWERS

4 Assemble the flowers. Insert a posy pick into the top tier and place the handle of the larger spray into it. Position the smaller spray at the base of the cake to balance the design.

Chasing rainbows

The colourful braid around the base of the cake was the inspiration for this cute birthday cake. This design illustrates that you do not need to use many flowers on a cake to create a pretty design.

MATERIALS

15-cm (6-in) round rich fruitcake
Apricot glaze
Icing sugar
350 g (12 oz) white almond paste
Clear alcohol (Cointreau or Kirsch)
450 g (1 lb) white sugarpaste, to cover cake and board
White royal icing
Multicoloured daisy braid, to trim the cake
Broad silver satin ribbon, to trim the board
Non-toxic glue stick (Pritt) (or a couple of large corsage pins)
Nile green floristry tape
Pink, blue, orange, purple, green and yellow paper-covered wires

EQUIPMENT

15-cm (6-in) thin round cake card
Pastry brush
Non-stick large rolling pin
Make-up sponge
Sugarpaste smoothers
23-cm (9-in) round cake board
Sharp knife
Piping bag and no. 42 rope piping tube
Fine-nose pliers
Posy pick

FLOWERS

1 rangoon creeper (see pages 74–5)

PREPARATION

1 Place the cake on the cake card. Brush the cake with warmed apricot glaze and cover with almond paste. Allow to dry overnight if time allows. Use a make-up sponge to moisten the surface of the almond paste with clear alcohol and then cover with white sugarpaste. Use sugarpaste smoothers to create a smooth, neat finish. Allow to dry.

2 Cover the cake board with white sugarpaste. Trim off the excess using a sharp knife and then position the cake centrally on top. Use a straight-edged smoother to create a neat join between the cake and the board. Allow to dry.

DECORATION

3 Fit a piping bag with a no. 42 rope piping tube and fill with white royal icing. Pipe a shell border around the base of the cake. Allow to dry. Attach a band of colourful braid above the piped border using a small amount of royal icing at the back of the cake.

4 Secure a band of silver satin ribbon to the board edge using a non-toxic glue stick or a couple of large corsage pins.

FLOWERS

5 Take several lengths of multicoloured paper-covered wires and twist together at one end. Create an open loop and then start to plait the remaining length together to form a long tail. Add the large rose to form the focal point of the spray. Complete the display with the rangoon creeper flowers and foliage. Insert a posy pick into the cake and place the handle of the spray into it. Reshape the plaited wires if needed.

Objects of desire

Roses are desired by many brides for bouquets and wedding cakes. Here is a perfect example of a cake design often requested by brides – calm, uncluttered and in pretty pastel colours. However, I have added a twist to the design by using very exotic and unusual secondary flowers – pink masdevallia orchids, tillandsia flowers and foliage and blue clerodendron – just to satisfy my desire to create something different and interesting!

MATERIALS

15-cm (6-in) and 23-cm (9-in) round rich fruitcakes
Apricot glaze
Icing sugar
1.4 kg (3 lb) white almond paste
Clear alcohol (kirsch or Cointreau)
1.8 kg (4 lb) champagne sugarpaste, to cover cakes and larger board
Broad satin lime green ribbon, to trim baseboard
Non-toxic glue stick or corsage pins
Decorative twisted braid, to trim the cakes
Small amount of royal icing (optional)

EQUIPMENT

15-cm (6-in) and 23-cm (9-in) thin round cake boards and 35-cm (14-in) round cake board
Pastry brush
Rolling pin
Sugarpaste smoothers
Make-up sponge
Perspex dowels
15-cm (6-in) perspex separator
2 posy picks

FLOWERS

2 large white roses (see pages 18–21)
1 half rose (see pages 18–21)
2 rosebuds (see pages 18–21)
10 blue butterfly flowers (see page 78)
3 pink masdevallia orchids (see page 79)
5 tillandsia flowers and foliage (see page 81)
3 bromeliad leaves (see page 80)
10 beetleweed leaves (see page 72)

PREPARATION

1 Place the cakes onto the same-sized thin boards. Brush them with warmed apricot glaze and cover with white almond paste. Use sugarpaste smoothers to create a neat, polished surface. Leave to dry overnight. Moisten the surface of the almond paste with clear alcohol using a make-up sponge and cover with champagne sugarpaste. Store the smaller cake on a sheet of greaseproof paper until dry. In the meantime, cover the large round board with sugarpaste and transfer the larger cake on top. Use smoothers to neaten the join at the base of the cake and to polish the top surface of the cake. Leave to dry. Attach a band of lime green ribbon to the edge of the baseboard using a non-toxic glue stick or corsage pins.

2 Insert three perspex dowels into the centre of the large tier and trim off the excess. The dowels help to support the weight of the separator and the top tier. Place the separator centrally on top of the large cake and place the small cake on top of it.

ASSEMBLY/SPRAYS

3 The following instructions are for the larger spray. The smaller one is made in a similar way using fewer flowers. Tape a half rose and rosebud onto either side of the large rose using half-width nile green tape. Next, add the blue butterfly bush flowers to create a line running through the spray. Add the masdevallia orchids and tillandsia flowers and foliage to soften the edges. Encircle the flowers with the beetleweed and bromeliad foliage.

4 Attach a band of decorative braid around the base of both cakes using a tiny amount of royal icing or softened sugarpaste/clear alcohol mix. Insert a posy pick into each cake and position a spray into each one.

CAKES

Green fingers

I love combining different textures of green flowers and foliage. This unusual curved, heart-shaped cake would be ideal for anyone blessed with green fingers! The finger-like quality of the spider chrysanthemum and the tiny leaves of the trailing succulents help to soften the more architectural form of the upright pitcher plant.

MATERIALS

15-cm (6-in) curved heart-shaped rich fruitcake

Apricot glaze

450 g (1 lb) white almond paste

Icing sugar

Clear alcohol (Cointreau or kirsch)

450 g (1 lb) white sugarpaste

Cocoa butter

Vine, moss, foliage and aubergine petal dusts

Fine pale green ribbon, to trim the base of the cake

EQUIPMENT

15-cm (6-in) curved heart-shaped thin cake board

Pastry brush

Non-stick rolling pin

Make-up sponge

Sugarpaste smoothers

Green fingers template (page 142)

Greaseproof or tracing paper

Sharp pencil

Icing scriber or a biro that has run dry

Mug and saucer

Fine paintbrushes

23-cm (9-in) rustic wooden dish

Florists' staysoft

Fine-nose pliers

Wire cutters

FLOWERS

1 green spider chrysanthemum (see pages 34–5)

3 pitcher plants (see page 36)

3 groups of cotinus foliage (see page 47)

3 bromeliad leaves (see page 80)

3 beetleweed leaves (see page 72)

10 stems of trailing succulents (see page 45)

PREPARATION

1 Place the cake on the board. Brush the cake with warmed apricot glaze and cover with almond paste. Leave to dry overnight. Moisten the surface of the almond paste with clear alcohol using a make-up sponge. Cover the cake with the sugarpaste, carefully easing the paste over the point of the heart shape. Use the sugarpaste smoothers to create a neat finish. Allow to dry overnight. Attach a band of fine pale green ribbon to the bottom edge of the cake using a small amount of royal icing or softened sugarpaste.

COCOA-PAINTED DESIGN

2 Trace the curved leaf design on to greaseproof or tracing paper using a sharp pencil. Place the tracing on top of the cake and scribe the design carefully on to the surface of the cake using an icing scriber or, better still, a biro pen that has run out of ink.

3 Place a small amount of grated cocoa butter on to a saucer and place over a mug of just boiled water to melt it. Add small amounts of vine green petal dust to the melted cocoa butter to make a paint. Start painting the design on to the cake using a fine paintbrush. Gradually build up the design, adding darker green petal dusts and finally defining the shapes with aubergine. Allow each layer of cocoa butter paint to set before adding the next layer – this does not take too long if the room that you are working in is not too hot.

ASSEMBLY

4 Place the cake on top of the rustic wooden dish. Tilt the cake slightly using some leftover almond paste or staysoft. Attach a lump of staysoft at the front of the cake, making sure that it does not directly touch the side of the cake. Using fine-nose pliers, bend a hook in the wired stem of the spider chrysanthemum – this will add extra support when it is pushed into the staysoft. Add the three pitchers and the groups of cotinus foliage to frame the focal chrysanthemum flower. Fill in the gaps with the bromeliad and beetleweed leaves. Finally, add the trailing succulent stems to the arrangement and also wrap some more stems around the base of the cake to complete the design.

Gilded lily

An unusual colourful combination of golden spider lilies, sandersonia and deep pink open roses adorn this two-tier wedding cake. A gold braid forms a very quick and effective decoration to the cake and the baseboard.

MATERIALS

15-cm (6-in) and 23-cm (9-in) round rich
  fruitcakes
Apricot glaze
Icing sugar
1.4 kg (3 lb) white almond paste
Clear alcohol (kirsch or Cointreau)
1.8 kg (4 lb) champagne sugarpaste,
  to cover cakes and larger board
Antique gold braid, to trim the cakes
  and the baseboard
Small amount of royal icing (optional)
Golden yellow ribbon, to trim baseboard
Non-toxic glue stick
Corsage pins
White flowerpaste
Edible gold and silver leaf
Plum, coral and foliage green petal dusts
Green florists' staysoft
Gold paper-covered reel wire

EQUIPMENT

15-cm (6-in) and 23-cm (9-in) thin round
  cake boards and a 35-cm (14-in) round
  cake board
Pastry brush
Rolling pin
Sugarpaste smoothers
Make-up sponge
Paisley paper punch
Fine paintbrush
2 small ceramic dishes
Fine-nose pliers
Wire cutters

FLOWERS

5 stems of sandersonia (see pages 50–1)
3 full-blown roses and 1 rosebud
  (see pages 52–4)
3 golden spider lilies (see pages 82–3)
2 sets of rose leaves (see pages 18–21)
6 stems of Geraldton waxplant flowers
  (see page 77)
3 bromeliad leaves (see page 80)

PREPARATION

1 Place the cakes onto the same-sized thin boards. Brush the cakes with warmed apricot glaze and cover with white almond paste. Use sugarpaste smoothers to create a neat, polished surface. Leave to dry overnight. Moisten the surface of the almond paste with clear alcohol using a make-up sponge and cover with champagne sugarpaste. Cover the large round board with sugarpaste and transfer the larger cake on top. Use smoothers to neaten the join at the base of the cake and to polish the top surface of the cake. Place the smaller cake on top of the large cake, again blending and tidying the join around the base of the cake using the straight-edged smoother. Leave to dry.

2 Attach a band of antique gold braid around the base of both cakes using a tiny amount of royal icing or softened sugarpaste/clear alcohol mix. Attach a band of golden yellow ribbon to the edge of the baseboard using a non-toxic glue stick. Pin a band of gold braid over the top of the ribbon using corsage pins.

SIDE DESIGN

3 Using the paisley paper punch cut out gold and silver leaf-coated shapes from white flowerpaste (see Crowing glory on pages 116–7). Attach to the sides of the cake using a little clear alcohol. For some extra detail add highlight dots using each of these colours in turn – plum, coral and foliage green mixed with clear alcohol, painted with a fine paintbrush.

FLOWERS

4 Fill the small ceramic dishes with green florists' staysoft. Using fine-nose pliers, hook the long stems of sandersonia and insert them into the staysoft to create the height, length and shape of the arrangements. Add the roses to create the focal area, followed by the golden spider lilies – be very careful when arranging them as their petals can be very fragile. Insert the rose leaves, wax flowers and bromeliad foliage to fill in the gaps and add interest. Add a series of large gold paper-covered wire loops to the left of the top arrangement.

Silver trail

Using a large posy of flowers on top of a fairly small cake makes a very bold statement that requires plenty of space in the rest of the cake design. The silver cut-out leaves at the base of the cake and the trails of metallic crimped wires help to balance and also soften the design as a whole.

MATERIALS
18-cm (7-in) round fruitcake
Apricot glaze
750 g (1 lb 10 oz) white almond paste
Icing sugar
Clear alcohol (Cointreau or kirsch)
900 g (2 lb) white sugarpaste, to cover
    cake and larger board
White royal icing
White satin ribbon, to trim cake board
Non-toxic glue stick (Pritt) (or large
    corsage pins)
White flowerpaste
Edible silver leaf (SK)
Pale blue pearl dragées
Vine, foliage and white petal dusts

EQUIPMENT
18-cm (7-in) round thin cake board
Pastry brush
Large non-stick rolling pin
Sugarpaste smoothers
Make-up sponge
25-cm (10-in) round cake board
Piping bag and no. 42 piping tube
Non-stick board
Small non-stick rolling pin
Monstera leaf paper punch
Fine paintbrush
Posy pick

FLOWERS
Silver trail posy (see pages 96–7)

PREPARATION

1 Place the cake on to the cake board of the same size. Brush the cake with warmed apricot glaze and cover with almond paste. Leave to dry overnight. Moisten the surface of the almond paste with clear alcohol using a make-up sponge and cover with sugarpaste. Use the smoothers to create a neat result. Lightly moisten the second cake board with clear alcohol and cover with a layer of white sugarpaste. Transfer the coated cake to the covered board and blend the bottom edge of the cake to the board with the straight-edged smoother. Leave to dry overnight.

2 Using a piping bag fitted with a no. 42 tube and filled with white royal icing, pipe a small shell trail around the base of the cake. Leave to set for a few hours. Attach a band of white satin ribbon to the edge of the board using non-toxic glue stick or corsage pins.

SILVER LEAVES

3 Roll out a small amount of well-kneaded white flowerpaste very thinly on to a non-stick board. Peel back the paste to reveal the sticky side. Place the sticky side of the paste on top of a sheet of silver leaf. Rub over the paste to secure the two mediums together. Turn the paste over to reveal the silver side and trim away any excess paste from the edges. Allow the paste to rest for about 10 or 20 minutes before using it in the paper punch.

4 Cut out several monstera leaves using the paper punch. Cut out extras to use at a later stage as the silver is expensive, so you really should not waste any. Allow the leaves to dry.

5 Attach the silver leaves at intervals around the base of the cake using tiny amounts of royal icing. Place a single pale blue pearl dragée on each silver leaf and secure with a tiny dot of royal icing.

6 Mix a 'paint' using vine, foliage and white petal dusts diluted with clear alcohol. Paint a few dots on each leaf using a fine paintbrush.

ASSEMBLY

7 Insert a posy pick into the cake and place the posy handle into it to settle the flowers in place. Angle the posy slightly and reshape any of the flower or wire components as required.

Summer breeze

This beautiful three-tier wedding cake adorned with delicate sprays of gardenias, orchids, ruscus and gold curls would be ideal for summer nuptials – all that is missing is the exquisite scent of fresh gardenias! If you are decide to use sponge cakes or a combination of fruitcakes and sponge cakes you will need to dowel each layer of the cake. I usually use dummy cakes when creating a stacked cake as they are very heavy to lift.

MATERIALS

13-cm (5-in), 20-cm (8-in) and 28-cm (11in) round rich fruitcakes
Apricot glaze
Icing sugar
3 kg (6 lb) white almond paste
5 kg (10 lb) white sugarpaste, to cover baseboard and cakes
Clear alcohol (kirsch or Cointreau)
Gold organza ribbon, to trim the cakes
Green and gold braid, to double trim the cakes
Small amount of royal icing (optional)
Green velvet ribbon, to trim the baseboard
Non-toxic glue stick (Pritt) or corsage pins
Cocoa butter
Vine green and foliage petal dusts

EQUIPMENT

13-cm (5-in), 20-cm (8-in) and 28-cm (11-in) round thin cake cards
Pastry brush
Rolling pin
Sugarpaste smoothers
40-cm (16-in) round cake board
Make-up sponge
Saucer and mug
Fine paintbrush
3 posy picks

FLOWERS

5 large gardenias (see pages 40–3)
3 half gardenias (see pages 40–3)
3 gardenia buds (see pages 40–3)
15 sprigs of smilax (see page 46)
20 gardenia leaves (see pages 40–3)
6 eyelash orchids (see pages 56–7)

PREPARATION

1 Place the three cakes onto their matching thin cake cards. Brush the cakes with warmed apricot glaze and then cover each one with a layer of white almond paste. Use a curved smoother on the top of the cakes and a straight-edged smoother on the sides to create a neat join at the base of each cake. Leave to dry overnight.

2 Lightly moisten and cover the large baseboard with a layer of white sugarpaste.

3 Use a make-up sponge to apply a thin coat of clear alcohol onto the almond paste on each cake. Cover each cake with white sugarpaste. Use smoothers to create a neat finish. A pad of well-kneaded sugarpaste pressed in the palm of your hand will help to create a more polished finish.

4 Place the largest cake onto the baseboard. Use the straight-edged smoother to neaten and bond the edge of the cake with the board.

ASSEMBLY

5 Attach a band of gold organza ribbon around the base of each cake using royal icing or a small amount of softened sugarpaste. Double the impact with a layer of green and gold braid. Attach a band of green velvet ribbon to the board edge using non-toxic glue or corsage pins.

6 Melt a small amount of cocoa butter on a saucer over a mug of just boiled water. Mix in some vine and foliage green petal dusts to make a pale green paint. Use a fine paintbrush to add a trailing dotted design at intervals around the three tiers and to the baseboard.

CAKES

SPRAY ASSEMBLY

7 These instructions are for the largest spray. Group together the large gardenia flowers using the largest, prettiest flower at the centre to create the focal point. Tape together using half-width nile green floristry tape. Add the half gardenia flowers and buds towards the edges of the spray. Next, add the smilax leaves around the flowers and create two extensions of this foliage to create an 'S' shape to the spray. Bulk out the spray with the gardenia foliage and finally add the eyelash orchids, taking care as the petals are very fragile. To complete the display, add trails of gold paper-covered wire. Insert the posy picks and sprays in the following positions: the large spray in the top cake, the medium spray in the top of the bottom tier and the small spray in the side at the base of the bottom tier.

Exotica

Exotic orchid tree flowers are perfectly combined with Heart's Desire and Eyelash orchids on this eye-catching cake that would be suitable for a small pearl wedding anniversary or birthday cake.

MATERIALS

15-cm (6-in) round rich fruitcake
Apricot glaze
Icing sugar
350 g (12 oz) white almond paste
Clear alcohol (Cointreau or kirsch)
350 g (12 oz) pink sugarpaste
Fine pink satin ribbon, to trim the cakes
Small amount of royal icing (optional)
Florists' silver mesh wire
Nile green floristry tape
Posy pick
5 pearl-like beads
Green crimped reel wire

EQUIPMENT

15-cm (6-in) thin round cake board
Pastry brush
Rolling pin
Sugarpaste smoothers
Make-up sponge
Wire cutters or sharp scissors
Fine-nose pliers

FLOWERS

2 heart's desire orchids (see pages 22–4)
6 eyelash orchids (see pages 56–7)
2 orchid tree flowers and foliage
  (see pages 30–2)
5 green begonia leaves (see page 28)
5 stems of trailing succulents
  (see page 45)
3 stems of wire vine (see page 84)

PREPARATION

1 Place the cake onto the board and then brush the surface with warmed apricot glaze. Cover the cake with almond paste and leave to dry overnight. Moisten the surface of the almond paste with clear alcohol using a make-up sponge and cover with pink sugarpaste. Use the curved smoother to create a smooth surface on the top of the cake and the straight-edged smoother to create a neat baseline around the cake. Allow to dry.

2 Attach a band of pink ribbon around the base of the cake securing it with a tiny amount of royal icing or a softened sugarpaste/clear alcohol mixture of the same sort of consistency. Elevate the cake a little using a solid glass tealight holder (or something similar). Wrap a tangled length of florists silver mesh wire loosely around the base of the cake leaving a trail to the right hand side. Trim off the excess wire using wire cutters or sharp scissors.

FLOWERS

3 Tape together the two small sprays (one slightly larger than the other) using half-width nile green floristry tape. Use the heart's desire orchids as the focal point of each spray. Gradually build up the spray around the orchid using the eyelash orchids and orchid tree flowers. Add the begonia leaves to really fill out the shape of each spray and use the trailing succulents and wire vine to soften the edges. Add a trail of the silver mesh wire to flow through the spray and tape securely into place.

4 Insert a posy pick into the cake and slide the handle of the spray into it. Readjust any flowers as necessary. Position the smaller spray against the mesh at the base of the cake and then simply tie the pearl beads onto the mesh and the odd leaf stem using green crimped wire.

Templates

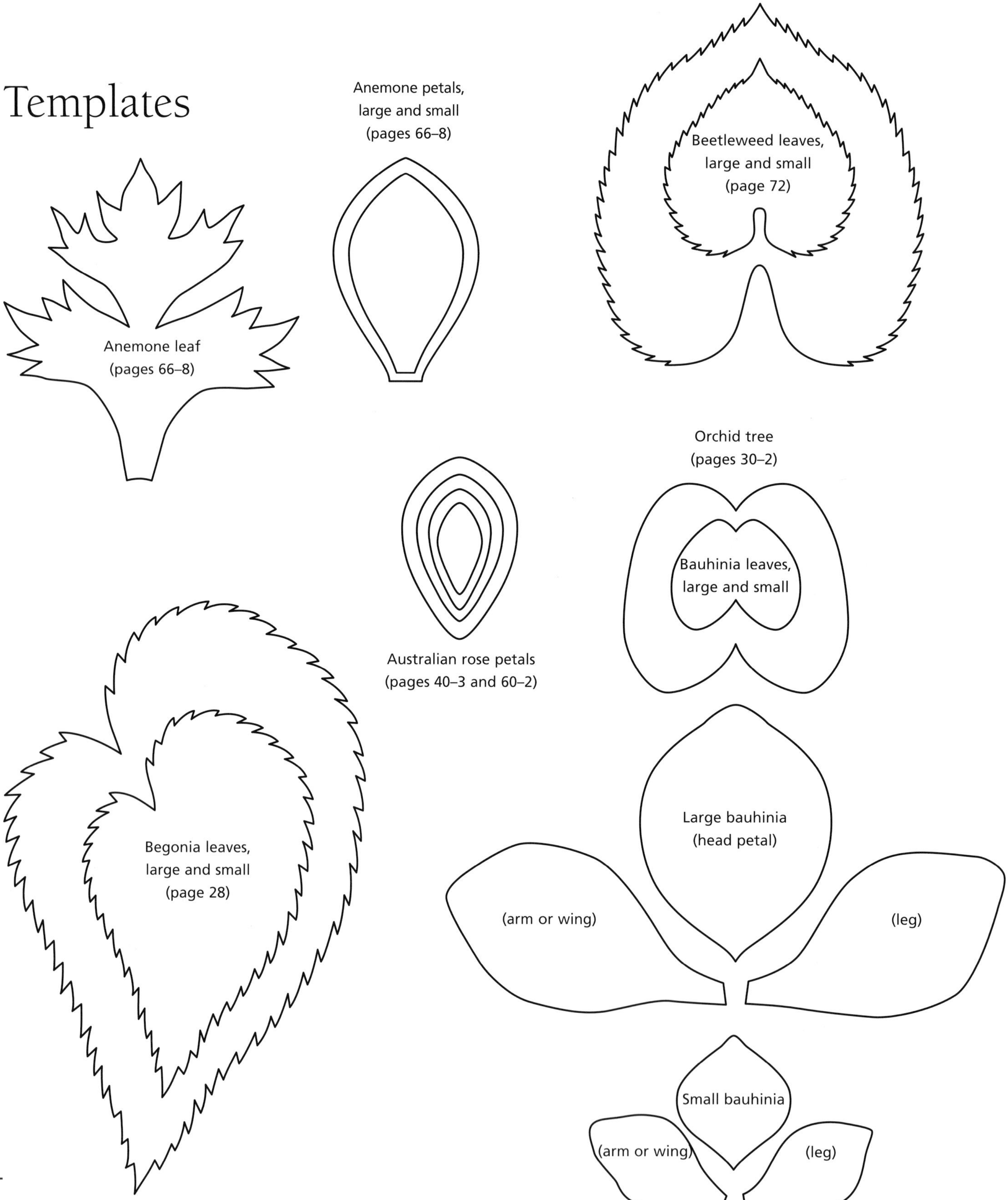

Anemone petals,
large and small
(pages 66–8)

Beetleweed leaves,
large and small
(page 72)

Anemone leaf
(pages 66–8)

Orchid tree
(pages 30–2)

Bauhinia leaves,
large and small

Australian rose petals
(pages 40–3 and 60–2)

Large bauhinia
(head petal)

Begonia leaves,
large and small
(page 28)

(arm or wing)

(leg)

Small bauhinia

(arm or wing)

(leg)

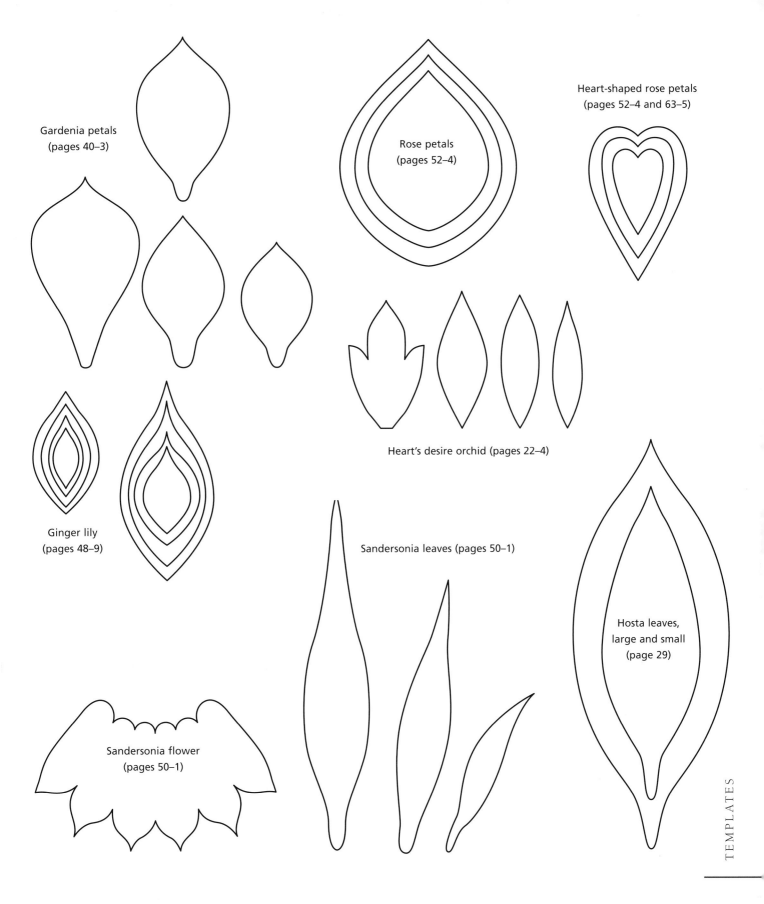

Gardenia petals
(pages 40–3)

Rose petals
(pages 52–4)

Heart-shaped rose petals
(pages 52–4 and 63–5)

Heart's desire orchid (pages 22–4)

Ginger lily
(pages 48–9)

Sandersonia leaves (pages 50–1)

Hosta leaves,
large and small
(page 29)

Sandersonia flower
(pages 50–1)

TEMPLATES

141

Green fingers (pages 130–32)

Gothica shoe
(pages 98–9)

Pitcher plant
(page 36)

Suppliers

www.alandunnsugarcraft.com

Aldaval Veiners (ALDV)
16 Chibburn Court
Widdrington
Morpeth
Northumberland NE61 5QT
allan@erhorn.fslife.co.uk

A Piece of Cake
18 Upper High Street
Thame
Oxon OX9 3EX
ww.apieceofcakethame.co.uk

Cakes, Classes and cutters
23 Princes Road
Brunton Park
Gosforth
Newcastle-upon-Tyne NE3 5TT
+44 (0)191 2170538

Cake Delights
219 High Street
Preston 3072
Melbourne
Australia

Celcakes and Celcrafts (Cc)
Springfield House
Gate Helmsley
York YO4 1NF
www.celcrafts.co.uk

Celebrations Teamvalley
Unit 383 G
Jedburgh Court
Team Valley Trading Estate
Gateshead
Tyne& Wear NE11 0BQ
www.celebrations-teamvalley.co.uk

Culpitt Cake Art
Jubilee Industrial Estate
Ashington
Northumberland NE63 8UG
+44 (0)1670 814545

Design-a-Cake
30/31 Phoenix Road
Crowther Industrial Estate
Washington
Tyne & Wear NE38 0AD
enquiry@design-a-cake.co.uk

Guy, Paul & Co. Ltd
Unit 10, The Business Centre
Corinium Industrial Estate
Raans Road
Amersham
Bucks HP6 6EB
sales@guypaul.co.uk

Holly Products (HP)
Primrose Cottage
Church Walk
Norton in Hales
Shropshire TF9 4QX
enquiries@hollyproducts.co.uk

Orchard Products (OPR)
51 Hallyburton Road
Hove
East Sussex BN3 7GP
+44 (0)1273 419418

Renshaw
Crown Street
Liverpool L8 7RF
+44 0870 870 6954

Squires Kitchen (SKGI)
Squires House
3 Waverley Lane
Farnham
Surrey GU9 8BB
www.squires-shop.com

The British Sugarcraft Guild
*for more information about
your nearest branch contact*:
Wellington House
Messeter Place
Eltham
London SE9 5DP
www.bsguk.org

The Old Bakery
Kingston St Mary
Taunton
Sommerset TA2 8HW
+44 (0)1823 451205

Tinkertech Two (TT)
40 Langdon Road
Parkstone
Poole
Dorset BH14 9EH
+44 (0)1202 738049

Wilton (W) and PME
Knightsbridge Bakeware
Centre Ltd
Chadwell Heath Lane
Romford
Essex RM6 4NP

Index

Dedicated to my folks: Allen, Avril and Susan.

INDEX/ACKNOWLEDGEMENTS

Huge thank yous to all of the following (in no particular order) for all of their help and kindness during the writing of this book. To Sue Atkinson and her assistant Edyta Girgiel for casting magical photography spells over my work, creating such beautiful images! To Corinne Masciocchi, my editor, for her help and direction and extreme patience. As always, my wonderful friends have been such a huge help and support to me in so many ways – too many to list here ! – so big hugs of gratitude and appreciation to Tombi Peck, Alice Christie, Tony Warren, Sathya, Chiyo Higashimura, Fumi Fukumuro, Alex and Martin Julian, Janet Berry, Ann Parker, John Quai Hoi, Kristofer Kerrigan-Graham, Christiane DuClos, Eileen Parkinson, Conor Day, Mary Jane Luke and anyone else I have forgotten! You are all stars! As always, the acknowledgements are written last in a dash!!!

Thank you also to the following for kindly supplying items for this book: Renshaws for all the Regalice used to coat the cakes, to Beverley Dutton of Squires Kitchen for being very generous with petal dusts, leaf veiners and gold and silver leaf, to Allan Erhorn for the dummy cakes and more leaf veiners, and to Norma Laver and Jenny Walker from A Piece of Cake for supplying the flowerpaste used to make many of the flowers in this book.